C-4267   CAREER EXAMINATION SERIES

This is your
PASSBOOK for...

Veterinary Technician

Test Preparation Study Guide
Questions & Answers

COPYRIGHT NOTICE

This book is SOLELY intended for, is sold ONLY to, and its use is RESTRICTED to individual, bona fide applicants or candidates who qualify by virtue of having seriously filed applications for appropriate license, certificate, professional and/or promotional advancement, higher school matriculation, scholarship, or other legitimate requirements of education and/or governmental authorities.

This book is NOT intended for use, class instruction, tutoring, training, duplication, copying, reprinting, excerption, or adaptation, etc., by:

1) Other publishers
2) Proprietors and/or Instructors of "Coaching" and/or Preparatory Courses
3) Personnel and/or Training Divisions of commercial, industrial, and governmental organizations
4) Schools, colleges, or universities and/or their departments and staffs, including teachers and other personnel
5) Testing Agencies or Bureaus
6) Study groups which seek by the purchase of a single volume to copy and/or duplicate and/or adapt this material for use by the group as a whole without having purchased individual volumes for each of the members of the group
7) Et al.

Such persons would be in violation of appropriate Federal and State statutes.

PROVISION OF LICENSING AGREEMENTS – Recognized educational, commercial, industrial, and governmental institutions and organizations, and others legitimately engaged in educational pursuits, including training, testing, and measurement activities, may address request for a licensing agreement to the copyright owners, who will determine whether, and under what conditions, including fees and charges, the materials in this book may be used them. In other words, a licensing facility exists for the legitimate use of the material in this book on other than an individual basis. However, it is asseverated and affirmed here that the material in this book CANNOT be used without the receipt of the express permission of such a licensing agreement from the Publishers. Inquiries re licensing should be addressed to the company, attention rights and permissions department.

All rights reserved, including the right of reproduction in whole or in part, in any form or by any means, electronic or mechanical, including photocopying, recording, or by any information storage and retrieval system, without permission in writing from the Publisher.

Copyright © 2024 by
National Learning Corporation

212 Michael Drive, Syosset, NY 11791
(516) 921-8888 • www.passbooks.com
E-mail: info@passbooks.com

PUBLISHED IN THE UNITED STATES OF AMERICA

PASSBOOK® SERIES

THE *PASSBOOK® SERIES* has been created to prepare applicants and candidates for the ultimate academic battlefield – the examination room.

At some time in our lives, each and every one of us may be required to take an examination – for validation, matriculation, admission, qualification, registration, certification, or licensure.

Based on the assumption that every applicant or candidate has met the basic formal educational standards, has taken the required number of courses, and read the necessary texts, the *PASSBOOK® SERIES* furnishes the one special preparation which may assure passing with confidence, instead of failing with insecurity. Examination questions – together with answers – are furnished as the basic vehicle for study so that the mysteries of the examination and its compounding difficulties may be eliminated or diminished by a sure method.

This book is meant to help you pass your examination provided that you qualify and are serious in your objective.

The entire field is reviewed through the huge store of content information which is succinctly presented through a provocative and challenging approach – the question-and-answer method.

A climate of success is established by furnishing the correct answers at the end of each test.

You soon learn to recognize types of questions, forms of questions, and patterns of questioning. You may even begin to anticipate expected outcomes.

You perceive that many questions are repeated or adapted so that you can gain acute insights, which may enable you to score many sure points.

You learn how to confront new questions, or types of questions, and to attack them confidently and work out the correct answers.

You note objectives and emphases, and recognize pitfalls and dangers, so that you may make positive educational adjustments.

Moreover, you are kept fully informed in relation to new concepts, methods, practices, and directions in the field.

You discover that you are actually taking the examination all the time: you are preparing for the examination by "taking" an examination, not by reading extraneous and/or supererogatory textbooks.

In short, this PASSBOOK®, used directedly, should be an important factor in helping you to pass your test.

VETERINARY TECHNICIANS

Veterinary Technicians are under the direct guidance and supervision of the veterinarian(s). Incumbents of this position are required to assist the practitioners to the fullest possible extent, to help improve the quality of care given to the patients of the veterinary center and to aid the practitioners in achieving greater efficiency by relieving them of technical work and administrative detail. In addition to the veterinarian(s), veterinary technicians report directly to the head technician.

MAJOR DUTIES:

- **In-Patient Medical Care**- give medications, assist or perform treatments, diagnostics & monitoring, place IV catheters, draw blood, run lab tests, administer IV fluids, cleaning, feeding, and walking patients as needed.
- **Anesthesia** induction, maintenance, monitoring, & recovery of patients, clean / maintain anesthesia equipment
- **Surgery**- Surgical prep, doctor assistance, clean, sterilize, and maintain all surgical instruments and OR equipment
- **Dentistry**- Provide patient dental care, ultrasonic cleaning and polishing, assist doctor with dental surgery, take dental radiographs
- **Radiology** (including dental imaging)- positioning patients and taking radiographs, submitting for consults
- **Laboratory duties**- collecting, preparing, & running or submitting samples for requested tests; reading and recording results when indicated (fecals, Urines, Ear cytology etc) when requested by doctor
- **Preparing invoices**, discharge instructions, and client information packs
- **Client communication**- give patient updates, discharge instructions, and provide followup for certain hospital patients.
- **Client medical demonstrations / education**
- **Technician appointments**- blood draws for therapeutic monitoring / screening tests, bandage changes, post-op checks, suture removals, AG, NT
- **Clinic technician**- assisting doctor with outpatient appointments, preparing, restocking, cleaning exam room, check patients in and out, take history and vitals, input date into patient medical record, ensure a smooth and timely flow of outpatient appointments from the check-in to the discharge
- **Assist with reception / front desk** duties as needed- answering phones, booking appointments, admit / discharge patients
- **Assist in training and mentoring** new team members
- **Assist with inventory control**, ordering, unpacking, restocking drug & medical supplies
- **Preparing prescriptions**, dispensed medications & medication refills

HOW TO TAKE A TEST

I. YOU MUST PASS AN EXAMINATION

A. WHAT EVERY CANDIDATE SHOULD KNOW

Examination applicants often ask us for help in preparing for the written test. What can I study in advance? What kinds of questions will be asked? How will the test be given? How will the papers be graded?

As an applicant for a civil service examination, you may be wondering about some of these things. Our purpose here is to suggest effective methods of advance study and to describe civil service examinations.

Your chances for success on this examination can be increased if you know how to prepare. Those "pre-examination jitters" can be reduced if you know what to expect. You can even experience an adventure in good citizenship if you know why civil service exams are given.

B. WHY ARE CIVIL SERVICE EXAMINATIONS GIVEN?

Civil service examinations are important to you in two ways. As a citizen, you want public jobs filled by employees who know how to do their work. As a job seeker, you want a fair chance to compete for that job on an equal footing with other candidates. The best-known means of accomplishing this two-fold goal is the competitive examination.

Exams are widely publicized throughout the nation. They may be administered for jobs in federal, state, city, municipal, town or village governments or agencies.

Any citizen may apply, with some limitations, such as the age or residence of applicants. Your experience and education may be reviewed to see whether you meet the requirements for the particular examination. When these requirements exist, they are reasonable and applied consistently to all applicants. Thus, a competitive examination may cause you some uneasiness now, but it is your privilege and safeguard.

C. HOW ARE CIVIL SERVICE EXAMS DEVELOPED?

Examinations are carefully written by trained technicians who are specialists in the field known as "psychological measurement," in consultation with recognized authorities in the field of work that the test will cover. These experts recommend the subject matter areas or skills to be tested; only those knowledges or skills important to your success on the job are included. The most reliable books and source materials available are used as references. Together, the experts and technicians judge the difficulty level of the questions.

Test technicians know how to phrase questions so that the problem is clearly stated. Their ethics do not permit "trick" or "catch" questions. Questions may have been tried out on sample groups, or subjected to statistical analysis, to determine their usefulness.

Written tests are often used in combination with performance tests, ratings of training and experience, and oral interviews. All of these measures combine to form the best-known means of finding the right person for the right job.

II. HOW TO PASS THE WRITTEN TEST

A. NATURE OF THE EXAMINATION

To prepare intelligently for civil service examinations, you should know how they differ from school examinations you have taken. In school you were assigned certain definite pages to read or subjects to cover. The examination questions were quite detailed and usually emphasized memory. Civil service exams, on the other hand, try to discover your present ability to perform the duties of a position, plus your potentiality to learn these duties. In other words, a civil service exam attempts to predict how successful you will be. Questions cover such a broad area that they cannot be as minute and detailed as school exam questions.

In the public service similar kinds of work, or positions, are grouped together in one "class." This process is known as *position-classification*. All the positions in a class are paid according to the salary range for that class. One class title covers all of these positions, and they are all tested by the same examination.

B. FOUR BASIC STEPS

1) Study the announcement

How, then, can you know what subjects to study? Our best answer is: "Learn as much as possible about the class of positions for which you've applied." The exam will test the knowledge, skills and abilities needed to do the work.

Your most valuable source of information about the position you want is the official exam announcement. This announcement lists the training and experience qualifications. Check these standards and apply only if you come reasonably close to meeting them.

The brief description of the position in the examination announcement offers some clues to the subjects which will be tested. Think about the job itself. Review the duties in your mind. Can you perform them, or are there some in which you are rusty? Fill in the blank spots in your preparation.

Many jurisdictions preview the written test in the exam announcement by including a section called "Knowledge and Abilities Required," "Scope of the Examination," or some similar heading. Here you will find out specifically what fields will be tested.

2) Review your own background

Once you learn in general what the position is all about, and what you need to know to do the work, ask yourself which subjects you already know fairly well and which need improvement. You may wonder whether to concentrate on improving your strong areas or on building some background in your fields of weakness. When the announcement has specified "some knowledge" or "considerable knowledge," or has used adjectives like "beginning principles of..." or "advanced ... methods," you can get a clue as to the number and difficulty of questions to be asked in any given field. More questions, and hence broader coverage, would be included for those subjects which are more important in the work. Now weigh your strengths and weaknesses against the job requirements and prepare accordingly.

3) Determine the level of the position

Another way to tell how intensively you should prepare is to understand the level of the job for which you are applying. Is it the entering level? In other words, is this the position in which beginners in a field of work are hired? Or is it an intermediate or advanced level? Sometimes this is indicated by such words as "Junior" or "Senior" in the class title. Other jurisdictions use Roman numerals to designate the level – Clerk I, Clerk II, for example. The word "Supervisor" sometimes appears in the title. If the level is not indicated by the title, check the description of duties. Will you be working under very close supervision, or will you have responsibility for independent decisions in this work?

4) Choose appropriate study materials

Now that you know the subjects to be examined and the relative amount of each subject to be covered, you can choose suitable study materials. For beginning level jobs, or even advanced ones, if you have a pronounced weakness in some aspect of your training, read a modern, standard textbook in that field. Be sure it is up to date and has general coverage. Such books are normally available at your library, and the librarian will be glad to help you locate one. For entry-level positions, questions of appropriate difficulty are chosen – neither highly advanced questions, nor those too simple. Such questions require careful thought but not advanced training.

If the position for which you are applying is technical or advanced, you will read more advanced, specialized material. If you are already familiar with the basic principles of your field, elementary textbooks would waste your time. Concentrate on advanced textbooks and technical periodicals. Think through the concepts and review difficult problems in your field.

These are all general sources. You can get more ideas on your own initiative, following these leads. For example, training manuals and publications of the government agency which employs workers in your field can be useful, particularly for technical and professional positions. A letter or visit to the government department involved may result in more specific study suggestions, and certainly will provide you with a more definite idea of the exact nature of the position you are seeking.

III. KINDS OF TESTS

Tests are used for purposes other than measuring knowledge and ability to perform specified duties. For some positions, it is equally important to test ability to make adjustments to new situations or to profit from training. In others, basic mental abilities not dependent on information are essential. Questions which test these things may not appear as pertinent to the duties of the position as those which test for knowledge and information. Yet they are often highly important parts of a fair examination. For very general questions, it is almost impossible to help you direct your study efforts. What we can do is to point out some of the more common of these general abilities needed in public service positions and describe some typical questions.

1) General information

Broad, general information has been found useful for predicting job success in some kinds of work. This is tested in a variety of ways, from vocabulary lists to questions about current events. Basic background in some field of work, such as sociology or economics, may be sampled in a group of questions. Often these are principles which have become familiar to most persons through exposure rather than through formal training. It is difficult to advise you how to study for these questions; being alert to the world around you is our best suggestion.

2) Verbal ability

An example of an ability needed in many positions is verbal or language ability. Verbal ability is, in brief, the ability to use and understand words. Vocabulary and grammar tests are typical measures of this ability. Reading comprehension or paragraph interpretation questions are common in many kinds of civil service tests. You are given a paragraph of written material and asked to find its central meaning.

3) Numerical ability

Number skills can be tested by the familiar arithmetic problem, by checking paired lists of numbers to see which are alike and which are different, or by interpreting charts and graphs. In the latter test, a graph may be printed in the test booklet which you are asked to use as the basis for answering questions.

4) Observation

A popular test for law-enforcement positions is the observation test. A picture is shown to you for several minutes, then taken away. Questions about the picture test your ability to observe both details and larger elements.

5) Following directions

In many positions in the public service, the employee must be able to carry out written instructions dependably and accurately. You may be given a chart with several columns, each column listing a variety of information. The questions require you to carry out directions involving the information given in the chart.

6) Skills and aptitudes

Performance tests effectively measure some manual skills and aptitudes. When the skill is one in which you are trained, such as typing or shorthand, you can practice. These tests are often very much like those given in business school or high school courses. For many of the other skills and aptitudes, however, no short-time preparation can be made. Skills and abilities natural to you or that you have developed throughout your lifetime are being tested.

Many of the general questions just described provide all the data needed to answer the questions and ask you to use your reasoning ability to find the answers. Your best preparation for these tests, as well as for tests of facts and ideas, is to be at your physical and mental best. You, no doubt, have your own methods of getting into an exam-taking mood and keeping "in shape." The next section lists some ideas on this subject.

IV. KINDS OF QUESTIONS

Only rarely is the "essay" question, which you answer in narrative form, used in civil service tests. Civil service tests are usually of the short-answer type. Full instructions for answering these questions will be given to you at the examination. But in case this is your first experience with short-answer questions and separate answer sheets, here is what you need to know:

1) Multiple-choice Questions

Most popular of the short-answer questions is the "multiple choice" or "best answer" question. It can be used, for example, to test for factual knowledge, ability to solve problems or judgment in meeting situations found at work.

A multiple-choice question is normally one of three types—
- It can begin with an incomplete statement followed by several possible endings. You are to find the one ending which *best* completes the statement, although some of the others may not be entirely wrong.
- It can also be a complete statement in the form of a question which is answered by choosing one of the statements listed.

- It can be in the form of a problem – again you select the best answer.

Here is an example of a multiple-choice question with a discussion which should give you some clues as to the method for choosing the right answer:

When an employee has a complaint about his assignment, the action which will *best* help him overcome his difficulty is to
- A. discuss his difficulty with his coworkers
- B. take the problem to the head of the organization
- C. take the problem to the person who gave him the assignment
- D. say nothing to anyone about his complaint

In answering this question, you should study each of the choices to find which is best. Consider choice "A" – Certainly an employee may discuss his complaint with fellow employees, but no change or improvement can result, and the complaint remains unresolved. Choice "B" is a poor choice since the head of the organization probably does not know what assignment you have been given, and taking your problem to him is known as "going over the head" of the supervisor. The supervisor, or person who made the assignment, is the person who can clarify it or correct any injustice. Choice "C" is, therefore, correct. To say nothing, as in choice "D," is unwise. Supervisors have and interest in knowing the problems employees are facing, and the employee is seeking a solution to his problem.

2) True/False Questions

The "true/false" or "right/wrong" form of question is sometimes used. Here a complete statement is given. Your job is to decide whether the statement is right or wrong.

SAMPLE: A roaming cell-phone call to a nearby city costs less than a non-roaming call to a distant city.

This statement is wrong, or false, since roaming calls are more expensive.

This is not a complete list of all possible question forms, although most of the others are variations of these common types. You will always get complete directions for answering questions. Be sure you understand *how* to mark your answers – ask questions until you do.

V. RECORDING YOUR ANSWERS

Computer terminals are used more and more today for many different kinds of exams.

For an examination with very few applicants, you may be told to record your answers in the test booklet itself. Separate answer sheets are much more common. If this separate answer sheet is to be scored by machine – and this is often the case – it is highly important that you mark your answers correctly in order to get credit.

An electronic scoring machine is often used in civil service offices because of the speed with which papers can be scored. Machine-scored answer sheets must be marked with a pencil, which will be given to you. This pencil has a high graphite content which responds to the electronic scoring machine. As a matter of fact, stray dots may register as answers, so do not let your pencil rest on the answer sheet while you are pondering the correct answer. Also, if your pencil lead breaks or is otherwise defective, ask for another.

Since the answer sheet will be dropped in a slot in the scoring machine, be careful not to bend the corners or get the paper crumpled.

The answer sheet normally has five vertical columns of numbers, with 30 numbers to a column. These numbers correspond to the question numbers in your test booklet. After each number, going across the page are four or five pairs of dotted lines. These short dotted lines have small letters or numbers above them. The first two pairs may also have a "T" or "F" above the letters. This indicates that the first two pairs only are to be used if the questions are of the true-false type. If the questions are multiple choice, disregard the "T" and "F" and pay attention only to the small letters or numbers.

Answer your questions in the manner of the sample that follows:

32. The largest city in the United States is
    A. Washington, D.C.
    B. New York City
    C. Chicago
    D. Detroit
    E. San Francisco

1) Choose the answer you think is best. (New York City is the largest, so "B" is correct.)
2) Find the row of dotted lines numbered the same as the question you are answering. (Find row number 32)
3) Find the pair of dotted lines corresponding to the answer. (Find the pair of lines under the mark "B.")
4) Make a solid black mark between the dotted lines.

VI. BEFORE THE TEST

Common sense will help you find procedures to follow to get ready for an examination. Too many of us, however, overlook these sensible measures. Indeed, nervousness and fatigue have been found to be the most serious reasons why applicants fail to do their best on civil service tests. Here is a list of reminders:

- Begin your preparation early – Don't wait until the last minute to go scurrying around for books and materials or to find out what the position is all about.
- Prepare continuously – An hour a night for a week is better than an all-night cram session. This has been definitely established. What is more, a night a week for a month will return better dividends than crowding your study into a shorter period of time.
- Locate the place of the exam – You have been sent a notice telling you when and where to report for the examination. If the location is in a different town or otherwise unfamiliar to you, it would be well to inquire the best route and learn something about the building.
- Relax the night before the test – Allow your mind to rest. Do not study at all that night. Plan some mild recreation or diversion; then go to bed early and get a good night's sleep.
- Get up early enough to make a leisurely trip to the place for the test – This way unforeseen events, traffic snarls, unfamiliar buildings, etc. will not upset you.
- Dress comfortably – A written test is not a fashion show. You will be known by number and not by name, so wear something comfortable.

- Leave excess paraphernalia at home – Shopping bags and odd bundles will get in your way. You need bring only the items mentioned in the official notice you received; usually everything you need is provided. Do not bring reference books to the exam. They will only confuse those last minutes and be taken away from you when in the test room.
- Arrive somewhat ahead of time – If because of transportation schedules you must get there very early, bring a newspaper or magazine to take your mind off yourself while waiting.
- Locate the examination room – When you have found the proper room, you will be directed to the seat or part of the room where you will sit. Sometimes you are given a sheet of instructions to read while you are waiting. Do not fill out any forms until you are told to do so; just read them and be prepared.
- Relax and prepare to listen to the instructions
- If you have any physical problem that may keep you from doing your best, be sure to tell the test administrator. If you are sick or in poor health, you really cannot do your best on the exam. You can come back and take the test some other time.

VII. AT THE TEST

The day of the test is here and you have the test booklet in your hand. The temptation to get going is very strong. Caution! There is more to success than knowing the right answers. You must know how to identify your papers and understand variations in the type of short-answer question used in this particular examination. Follow these suggestions for maximum results from your efforts:

1) Cooperate with the monitor

The test administrator has a duty to create a situation in which you can be as much at ease as possible. He will give instructions, tell you when to begin, check to see that you are marking your answer sheet correctly, and so on. He is not there to guard you, although he will see that your competitors do not take unfair advantage. He wants to help you do your best.

2) Listen to all instructions

Don't jump the gun! Wait until you understand all directions. In most civil service tests you get more time than you need to answer the questions. So don't be in a hurry. Read each word of instructions until you clearly understand the meaning. Study the examples, listen to all announcements and follow directions. Ask questions if you do not understand what to do.

3) Identify your papers

Civil service exams are usually identified by number only. You will be assigned a number; you must not put your name on your test papers. Be sure to copy your number correctly. Since more than one exam may be given, copy your exact examination title.

4) Plan your time

Unless you are told that a test is a "speed" or "rate of work" test, speed itself is usually not important. Time enough to answer all the questions will be provided, but this does not mean that you have all day. An overall time limit has been set. Divide the total time (in minutes) by the number of questions to determine the approximate time you have for each question.

5) Do not linger over difficult questions

If you come across a difficult question, mark it with a paper clip (useful to have along) and come back to it when you have been through the booklet. One caution if you do this – be sure to skip a number on your answer sheet as well. Check often to be sure that you have not lost your place and that you are marking in the row numbered the same as the question you are answering.

6) Read the questions

Be sure you know what the question asks! Many capable people are unsuccessful because they failed to *read* the questions correctly.

7) Answer all questions

Unless you have been instructed that a penalty will be deducted for incorrect answers, it is better to guess than to omit a question.

8) Speed tests

It is often better NOT to guess on speed tests. It has been found that on timed tests people are tempted to spend the last few seconds before time is called in marking answers at random – without even reading them – in the hope of picking up a few extra points. To discourage this practice, the instructions may warn you that your score will be "corrected" for guessing. That is, a penalty will be applied. The incorrect answers will be deducted from the correct ones, or some other penalty formula will be used.

9) Review your answers

If you finish before time is called, go back to the questions you guessed or omitted to give them further thought. Review other answers if you have time.

10) Return your test materials

If you are ready to leave before others have finished or time is called, take ALL your materials to the monitor and leave quietly. Never take any test material with you. The monitor can discover whose papers are not complete, and taking a test booklet may be grounds for disqualification.

VIII. EXAMINATION TECHNIQUES

1) Read the general instructions carefully. These are usually printed on the first page of the exam booklet. As a rule, these instructions refer to the timing of the examination; the fact that you should not start work until the signal and must stop work at a signal, etc. If there are any *special* instructions, such as a choice of questions to be answered, make sure that you note this instruction carefully.

2) When you are ready to start work on the examination, that is as soon as the signal has been given, read the instructions to each question booklet, underline any key words or phrases, such as *least*, *best*, *outline*, *describe* and the like. In this way you will tend to answer as requested rather than discover on reviewing your paper that you *listed without describing*, that you selected the *worst* choice rather than the *best* choice, etc.

3) If the examination is of the objective or multiple-choice type – that is, each question will also give a series of possible answers: A, B, C or D, and you are called upon to select the best answer and write the letter next to that answer on your answer paper – it is advisable to start answering each question in turn. There may be anywhere from 50 to 100 such questions in the three or four hours allotted and you can see how much time would be taken if you read through all the questions before beginning to answer any. Furthermore, if you come across a question or group of questions which you know would be difficult to answer, it would undoubtedly affect your handling of all the other questions.

4) If the examination is of the essay type and contains but a few questions, it is a moot point as to whether you should read all the questions before starting to answer any one. Of course, if you are given a choice – say five out of seven and the like – then it is essential to read all the questions so you can eliminate the two that are most difficult. If, however, you are asked to answer all the questions, there may be danger in trying to answer the easiest one first because you may find that you will spend too much time on it. The best technique is to answer the first question, then proceed to the second, etc.

5) Time your answers. Before the exam begins, write down the time it started, then add the time allowed for the examination and write down the time it must be completed, then divide the time available somewhat as follows:
    - If 3-1/2 hours are allowed, that would be 210 minutes. If you have 80 objective-type questions, that would be an average of 2-1/2 minutes per question. Allow yourself no more than 2 minutes per question, or a total of 160 minutes, which will permit about 50 minutes to review.
    - If for the time allotment of 210 minutes there are 7 essay questions to answer, that would average about 30 minutes a question. Give yourself only 25 minutes per question so that you have about 35 minutes to review.

6) The most important instruction is to *read each question* and make sure you know what is wanted. The second most important instruction is to *time yourself properly* so that you answer every question. The third most important instruction is to *answer every question*. Guess if you have to but include something for each question. Remember that you will receive no credit for a blank and will probably receive some credit if you write something in answer to an essay question. If you guess a letter – say "B" for a multiple-choice question – you may have guessed right. If you leave a blank as an answer to a multiple-choice question, the examiners may respect your feelings but it will not add a point to your score. Some exams may penalize you for wrong answers, so in such cases *only*, you may not want to guess unless you have some basis for your answer.

7) Suggestions
    a. Objective-type questions
        1. Examine the question booklet for proper sequence of pages and questions
        2. Read all instructions carefully
        3. Skip any question which seems too difficult; return to it after all other questions have been answered
        4. Apportion your time properly; do not spend too much time on any single question or group of questions

5. Note and underline key words – *all, most, fewest, least, best, worst, same, opposite*, etc.
6. Pay particular attention to negatives
7. Note unusual option, e.g., unduly long, short, complex, different or similar in content to the body of the question
8. Observe the use of "hedging" words – *probably, may, most likely*, etc.
9. Make sure that your answer is put next to the same number as the question
10. Do not second-guess unless you have good reason to believe the second answer is definitely more correct
11. Cross out original answer if you decide another answer is more accurate; do not erase until you are ready to hand your paper in
12. Answer all questions; guess unless instructed otherwise
13. Leave time for review

b. Essay questions
1. Read each question carefully
2. Determine exactly what is wanted. Underline key words or phrases.
3. Decide on outline or paragraph answer
4. Include many different points and elements unless asked to develop any one or two points or elements
5. Show impartiality by giving pros and cons unless directed to select one side only
6. Make and write down any assumptions you find necessary to answer the questions
7. Watch your English, grammar, punctuation and choice of words
8. Time your answers; don't crowd material

8) Answering the essay question

Most essay questions can be answered by framing the specific response around several key words or ideas. Here are a few such key words or ideas:

M's: manpower, materials, methods, money, management
P's: purpose, program, policy, plan, procedure, practice, problems, pitfalls, personnel, public relations

   a. Six basic steps in handling problems:
     1. Preliminary plan and background development
     2. Collect information, data and facts
     3. Analyze and interpret information, data and facts
     4. Analyze and develop solutions as well as make recommendations
     5. Prepare report and sell recommendations
     6. Install recommendations and follow up effectiveness

   b. Pitfalls to avoid
     1. *Taking things for granted* – A statement of the situation does not necessarily imply that each of the elements is necessarily true; for example, a complaint may be invalid and biased so that all that can be taken for granted is that a complaint has been registered

2. *Considering only one side of a situation* – Wherever possible, indicate several alternatives and then point out the reasons you selected the best one
3. *Failing to indicate follow up* – Whenever your answer indicates action on your part, make certain that you will take proper follow-up action to see how successful your recommendations, procedures or actions turn out to be
4. *Taking too long in answering any single question* – Remember to time your answers properly

IX. AFTER THE TEST

Scoring procedures differ in detail among civil service jurisdictions although the general principles are the same. Whether the papers are hand-scored or graded by machine we have described, they are nearly always graded by number. That is, the person who marks the paper knows only the number – never the name – of the applicant. Not until all the papers have been graded will they be matched with names. If other tests, such as training and experience or oral interview ratings have been given, scores will be combined. Different parts of the examination usually have different weights. For example, the written test might count 60 percent of the final grade, and a rating of training and experience 40 percent. In many jurisdictions, veterans will have a certain number of points added to their grades.

After the final grade has been determined, the names are placed in grade order and an eligible list is established. There are various methods for resolving ties between those who get the same final grade – probably the most common is to place first the name of the person whose application was received first. Job offers are made from the eligible list in the order the names appear on it. You will be notified of your grade and your rank as soon as all these computations have been made. This will be done as rapidly as possible.

People who are found to meet the requirements in the announcement are called "eligibles." Their names are put on a list of eligible candidates. An eligible's chances of getting a job depend on how high he stands on this list and how fast agencies are filling jobs from the list.

When a job is to be filled from a list of eligibles, the agency asks for the names of people on the list of eligibles for that job. When the civil service commission receives this request, it sends to the agency the names of the three people highest on this list. Or, if the job to be filled has specialized requirements, the office sends the agency the names of the top three persons who meet these requirements from the general list.

The appointing officer makes a choice from among the three people whose names were sent to him. If the selected person accepts the appointment, the names of the others are put back on the list to be considered for future openings.

That is the rule in hiring from all kinds of eligible lists, whether they are for typist, carpenter, chemist, or something else. For every vacancy, the appointing officer has his choice of any one of the top three eligibles on the list. This explains why the person whose name is on top of the list sometimes does not get an appointment when some of the persons lower on the list do. If the appointing officer chooses the second or third eligible, the No. 1 eligible does not get a job at once, but stays on the list until he is appointed or the list is terminated.

X. HOW TO PASS THE INTERVIEW TEST

The examination for which you applied requires an oral interview test. You have already taken the written test and you are now being called for the interview test – the final part of the formal examination.

You may think that it is not possible to prepare for an interview test and that there are no procedures to follow during an interview. Our purpose is to point out some things you can do in advance that will help you and some good rules to follow and pitfalls to avoid while you are being interviewed.

What is an interview supposed to test?

The written examination is designed to test the technical knowledge and competence of the candidate; the oral is designed to evaluate intangible qualities, not readily measured otherwise, and to establish a list showing the relative fitness of each candidate – as measured against his competitors – for the position sought. Scoring is not on the basis of "right" and "wrong," but on a sliding scale of values ranging from "not passable" to "outstanding." As a matter of fact, it is possible to achieve a relatively low score without a single "incorrect" answer because of evident weakness in the qualities being measured.

Occasionally, an examination may consist entirely of an oral test – either an individual or a group oral. In such cases, information is sought concerning the technical knowledges and abilities of the candidate, since there has been no written examination for this purpose. More commonly, however, an oral test is used to supplement a written examination.

Who conducts interviews?

The composition of oral boards varies among different jurisdictions. In nearly all, a representative of the personnel department serves as chairman. One of the members of the board may be a representative of the department in which the candidate would work. In some cases, "outside experts" are used, and, frequently, a businessman or some other representative of the general public is asked to serve. Labor and management or other special groups may be represented. The aim is to secure the services of experts in the appropriate field.

However the board is composed, it is a good idea (and not at all improper or unethical) to ascertain in advance of the interview who the members are and what groups they represent. When you are introduced to them, you will have some idea of their backgrounds and interests, and at least you will not stutter and stammer over their names.

What should be done before the interview?

While knowledge about the board members is useful and takes some of the surprise element out of the interview, there is other preparation which is more substantive. It *is* possible to prepare for an oral interview – in several ways:

1) Keep a copy of your application and review it carefully before the interview

This may be the only document before the oral board, and the starting point of the interview. Know what education and experience you have listed there, and the sequence and dates of all of it. Sometimes the board will ask you to review the highlights of your experience for them; you should not have to hem and haw doing it.

2) Study the class specification and the examination announcement

Usually, the oral board has one or both of these to guide them. The qualities, characteristics or knowledges required by the position sought are stated in these documents. They offer valuable clues as to the nature of the oral interview. For example, if the job involves supervisory responsibilities, the announcement will usually indicate that knowledge of modern supervisory methods and the qualifications of the candidate as a supervisor will be tested. If so, you can expect such questions, frequently in the form of a hypothetical situation which you are expected to solve. NEVER go into an oral without knowledge of the duties and responsibilities of the job you seek.

3) Think through each qualification required

Try to visualize the kind of questions you would ask if you were a board member. How well could you answer them? Try especially to appraise your own knowledge and background in each area, *measured against the job sought*, and identify any areas in which you are weak. Be critical and realistic – do not flatter yourself.

4) Do some general reading in areas in which you feel you may be weak

For example, if the job involves supervision and your past experience has NOT, some general reading in supervisory methods and practices, particularly in the field of human relations, might be useful. Do NOT study agency procedures or detailed manuals. The oral board will be testing your understanding and capacity, not your memory.

5) Get a good night's sleep and watch your general health and mental attitude

You will want a clear head at the interview. Take care of a cold or any other minor ailment, and of course, no hangovers.

What should be done on the day of the interview?

Now comes the day of the interview itself. Give yourself plenty of time to get there. Plan to arrive somewhat ahead of the scheduled time, particularly if your appointment is in the fore part of the day. If a previous candidate fails to appear, the board might be ready for you a bit early. By early afternoon an oral board is almost invariably behind schedule if there are many candidates, and you may have to wait. Take along a book or magazine to read, or your application to review, but leave any extraneous material in the waiting room when you go in for your interview. In any event, relax and compose yourself.

The matter of dress is important. The board is forming impressions about you – from your experience, your manners, your attitude, and your appearance. Give your personal appearance careful attention. Dress your best, but not your flashiest. Choose conservative, appropriate clothing, and be sure it is immaculate. This is a business interview, and your appearance should indicate that you regard it as such. Besides, being well groomed and properly dressed will help boost your confidence.

Sooner or later, someone will call your name and escort you into the interview room. *This is it.* From here on you are on your own. It is too late for any more preparation. But remember, you asked for this opportunity to prove your fitness, and you are here because your request was granted.

What happens when you go in?

The usual sequence of events will be as follows: The clerk (who is often the board stenographer) will introduce you to the chairman of the oral board, who will introduce you to the other members of the board. Acknowledge the introductions before you sit down. Do not be surprised if you find a microphone facing you or a stenotypist sitting by. Oral interviews are usually recorded in the event of an appeal or other review.

Usually the chairman of the board will open the interview by reviewing the highlights of your education and work experience from your application – primarily for the benefit of the other members of the board, as well as to get the material into the record. Do not interrupt or comment unless there is an error or significant misinterpretation; if that is the case, do not hesitate. But do not quibble about insignificant matters. Also, he will usually ask you some question about your education, experience or your present job – partly to get you to start talking and to establish the interviewing "rapport." He may start the actual questioning, or turn it over to one of the other members. Frequently, each member undertakes the questioning on a particular area, one in which he is perhaps most competent, so you can expect each member to participate in the examination. Because time is limited, you may also expect some rather abrupt switches in the direction the questioning takes, so do not be upset by it. Normally, a board member will not pursue a single line of questioning unless he discovers a particular strength or weakness.

After each member has participated, the chairman will usually ask whether any member has any further questions, then will ask you if you have anything you wish to add. Unless you are expecting this question, it may floor you. Worse, it may start you off on an extended, extemporaneous speech. The board is not usually seeking more information. The question is principally to offer you a last opportunity to present further qualifications or to indicate that you have nothing to add. So, if you feel that a significant qualification or characteristic has been overlooked, it is proper to point it out in a sentence or so. Do not compliment the board on the thoroughness of their examination – they have been sketchy, and you know it. If you wish, merely say, "No thank you, I have nothing further to add." This is a point where you can "talk yourself out" of a good impression or fail to present an important bit of information. Remember, *you close the interview yourself*.

The chairman will then say, "That is all, Mr. _____, thank you." Do not be startled; the interview is over, and quicker than you think. Thank him, gather your belongings and take your leave. Save your sigh of relief for the other side of the door.

How to put your best foot forward

Throughout this entire process, you may feel that the board individually and collectively is trying to pierce your defenses, seek out your hidden weaknesses and embarrass and confuse you. Actually, this is not true. They are obliged to make an appraisal of your qualifications for the job you are seeking, and they want to see you in your best light. Remember, they must interview all candidates and a non-cooperative candidate may become a failure in spite of their best efforts to bring out his qualifications. Here are 15 suggestions that will help you:

1) Be natural – Keep your attitude confident, not cocky

If you are not confident that you can do the job, do not expect the board to be. Do not apologize for your weaknesses, try to bring out your strong points. The board is interested in a positive, not negative, presentation. Cockiness will antagonize any board member and make him wonder if you are covering up a weakness by a false show of strength.

2) Get comfortable, but don't lounge or sprawl

Sit erectly but not stiffly. A careless posture may lead the board to conclude that you are careless in other things, or at least that you are not impressed by the importance of the occasion. Either conclusion is natural, even if incorrect. Do not fuss with your clothing, a pencil or an ashtray. Your hands may occasionally be useful to emphasize a point; do not let them become a point of distraction.

3) Do not wisecrack or make small talk

This is a serious situation, and your attitude should show that you consider it as such. Further, the time of the board is limited – they do not want to waste it, and neither should you.

4) Do not exaggerate your experience or abilities
   In the first place, from information in the application or other interviews and sources, the board may know more about you than you think. Secondly, you probably will not get away with it. An experienced board is rather adept at spotting such a situation, so do not take the chance.

5) If you know a board member, do not make a point of it, yet do not hide it
   Certainly you are not fooling him, and probably not the other members of the board. Do not try to take advantage of your acquaintanceship – it will probably do you little good.

6) Do not dominate the interview
   Let the board do that. They will give you the clues – do not assume that you have to do all the talking. Realize that the board has a number of questions to ask you, and do not try to take up all the interview time by showing off your extensive knowledge of the answer to the first one.

7) Be attentive
   You only have 20 minutes or so, and you should keep your attention at its sharpest throughout. When a member is addressing a problem or question to you, give him your undivided attention. Address your reply principally to him, but do not exclude the other board members.

8) Do not interrupt
   A board member may be stating a problem for you to analyze. He will ask you a question when the time comes. Let him state the problem, and wait for the question.

9) Make sure you understand the question
   Do not try to answer until you are sure what the question is. If it is not clear, restate it in your own words or ask the board member to clarify it for you. However, do not haggle about minor elements.

10) Reply promptly but not hastily
   A common entry on oral board rating sheets is "candidate responded readily," or "candidate hesitated in replies." Respond as promptly and quickly as you can, but do not jump to a hasty, ill-considered answer.

11) Do not be peremptory in your answers
   A brief answer is proper – but do not fire your answer back. That is a losing game from your point of view. The board member can probably ask questions much faster than you can answer them.

12) Do not try to create the answer you think the board member wants
   He is interested in what kind of mind you have and how it works – not in playing games. Furthermore, he can usually spot this practice and will actually grade you down on it.

13) Do not switch sides in your reply merely to agree with a board member
   Frequently, a member will take a contrary position merely to draw you out and to see if you are willing and able to defend your point of view. Do not start a debate, yet do not surrender a good position. If a position is worth taking, it is worth defending.

14) Do not be afraid to admit an error in judgment if you are shown to be wrong

The board knows that you are forced to reply without any opportunity for careful consideration. Your answer may be demonstrably wrong. If so, admit it and get on with the interview.

15) Do not dwell at length on your present job

The opening question may relate to your present assignment. Answer the question but do not go into an extended discussion. You are being examined for a *new* job, not your present one. As a matter of fact, try to phrase ALL your answers in terms of the job for which you are being examined.

Basis of Rating

Probably you will forget most of these "do's" and "don'ts" when you walk into the oral interview room. Even remembering them all will not ensure you a passing grade. Perhaps you did not have the qualifications in the first place. But remembering them will help you to put your best foot forward, without treading on the toes of the board members.

Rumor and popular opinion to the contrary notwithstanding, an oral board wants you to make the best appearance possible. They know you are under pressure – but they also want to see how you respond to it as a guide to what your reaction would be under the pressures of the job you seek. They will be influenced by the degree of poise you display, the personal traits you show and the manner in which you respond.

ABOUT THIS BOOK

This book contains tests divided into Examination Sections. Go through each test, answering every question in the margin. We have also attached a sample answer sheet at the back of the book that can be removed and used. At the end of each test look at the answer key and check your answers. On the ones you got wrong, look at the right answer choice and learn. Do not fill in the answers first. Do not memorize the questions and answers, but understand the answer and principles involved. On your test, the questions will likely be different from the samples. Questions are changed and new ones added. If you understand these past questions you should have success with any changes that arise. Tests may consist of several types of questions. We have additional books on each subject should more study be advisable or necessary for you. Finally, the more you study, the better prepared you will be. This book is intended to be the last thing you study before you walk into the examination room. Prior study of relevant texts is also recommended. NLC publishes some of these in our Fundamental Series. Knowledge and good sense are important factors in passing your exam. Good luck also helps. So now study this Passbook, absorb the material contained within and take that knowledge into the examination. Then do your best to pass that exam.

EXAMINATION SECTION

EXAMINATION SECTION
TEST 1

DIRECTIONS: Each question or incomplete statement is followed by several suggested answers or completions. Select the one that BEST answers the question or completes the statement. *PRINT THE LETTER OF THE CORRECT ANSWER IN THE SPACE AT THE RIGHT.*

1. What is the *most common* intestinal parasite in dogs? 1.____

    A. Ascarids B. Hookworms C. Protozoa
    D. Tapeworm E. Whipworm

2. All of the following are exclusively male diseases EXCEPT 2.____

    A. Phimosis B. Orchitis C. Balanoposthitis
    D. Pseudocyesis E. Cryptorchidism

3. What is the MAIN difference between the English Trim and Continental Trim? The 3.____

    A. rear leg hair is clipped to create bracelets in the English Trim
    B. Continental Trim shaves the front legs between the forearm and pastern
    C. Continental Trim clips the rear bare except for rosettes on the hips
    D. English Trim clips the tail to create a pom-pom at the tip
    E. English Trim clips the foot entirely

4. Which of the following is NOT a true statement? 4.____

    A. The dog cannot see colors
    B. The dog's visual field is greater than man's
    C. The dog is more sensitive to movement than man
    D. The dog is more sensitive to differences in brightness than man
    E. The dog can perform almost as well in total darkness as in a well-lighted room

5. *Most* older dogs die of 5.____

    A. cardiovascular disease B. cancer
    C. kidney disease D. bronchitis
    E. liver disease

6. Which one of the following inherited traits is *correctly* identified as dominant? 6.____

    A. Short hair is dominant over long hair
    B. A wire coat is dominant over a smooth coat
    C. Straight hair is dominant over curly hair
    D. A sparse coat is dominant over a dense coat
    E. Fine hair is dominant over coarse hair

7. The *oldest* American Sporting Dog is the 7.____

    A. American Foxhound B. Chesapeake Bay Retriever
    C. American Water Spaniel D. Field Spaniel
    E. Cocker Spaniel

8. What kind of hunting was the Dachshund used for? _____ hunting.

   A. Pheasant   B. Badger   C. Duck
   D. Possum   E. Partridge

9. What breed is said to have the build of a Terrier but the strength and agility of the finest Working Dogs?

   A. Great Dane   B. Great Pyrenees
   C. Giant Schnauzer   D. Newfoundland
   E. Rottweiler

10. What is the *most obvious* distinction between the Welsh Corgi, the Cardigan, and the Welsh Corgi, Pembroke?

    A. Coat color   B. Height and weight
    C. Tail and ears   D. Head and skull
    E. Height and length

11. Which of the following is *recommended* in persistently recurring cases of anal sac disease?

    A. Massage the sacs
    B. Antibiotics
    C. Injecting medication into the sacs
    D. Surgical drainage of the sacs
    E. Surgical removal of the sacs

12. Why should the number of dog biscuits fed to the dog be limited? They

    A. irritate the gums
    B. are difficult to digest
    C. are a source of calories
    D. cause cavities
    E. contribute to the recession of gum tissue

13. Which of the following are functions of the liver?
    I. Detoxification of poisons
    II. Aids in metabolism of fats
    III. Aids in clotting blood
    IV. Manufactures bile
    V. Storehouse for carbohydrates
    The CORRECT answer is:

    A. I, II, IV   B. II, III, IV, V   C. II, III, V
    D. All of the above   E. None of the above

14. All of the following are important during grooming EXCEPT:

    A. Groom the dog while he stands comfortably on the floor
    B. Be firm, and correct unwanted behavior
    C. Use the proper tools
    D. Make the experience pleasant for the dog
    E. Groom the dog in a closed, quiet room

15. An infectious disease of the urinary tract that is caused by germs is

    A. Chronic Canine Rhinitis B. Canine Brucellosis
    C. Leptospirosis D. Salmonellosis
    E. Hepatitis

16. How long should a suspected rabid dog who has bitten a a person be quarantined?

    A. One month B. One week C. Ten days
    D. Three months E. Six months

17. All of the following require laboratory diagnosis EXCEPT

    A. Glossitis B. Liver Disease
    C. Heartworm Disease D. Enteritis
    E. Acute Pancreatitis

18. Factors influencing the adult dog's diet include all of the following EXCEPT

    A. age B. variety C. lifestyle
    D. temperament E. breed

19. What is vital to hand-raising orphan puppies?

    A. Gradually reducing the temperature of their environment
    B. Helping the puppies urinate and defecate
    C. Using the proper milk substitute
    D. Keeping the puppies clean
    E. Keeping their environment clean

20. Recommended protein supplements are:
    I. Meat
    II. Cooked eggs
    III. III Farina
    IV. Milk
    V. Cottage cheese
    The CORRECT answer is:

    A. I, II, IV B. I, IV, V C. I, II, V
    D. I, II, IV, V E. All of the above

21. How may heat stroke be prevented?
    I. Adequate ventilation
    II. Limit food
    III. Available water
    IV. Enforce confinement
    V. Limit sun exposure
    The CORRECT answer is:

    A. I, II, III, V B. I, II, IV C. II, III, IV, V
    D. I, III, V E. All of the above

22. How can water consumption be effectively *increased*? By

    A. adding corn syrup to the water
    B. adding sugar to the water
    C. adding salt to the food
    D. adding sugar to the food
    E. exercising the dog

23. When taking a dog on a car trip,

    A. never leave the dog in a closed, locked car
    B. remove the leash but not the dog's collar
    C. feed the dog before leaving
    D. make sure the dog has water before leaving
    E. keep the dog in the back seat with a window open at least six inches

24. Which of the following is a reflex and *not* an insinct?

    A. The newborn puppy's nursing behavior
    B. Trail barking
    C. Mating behavior
    D. Pointing and retrieving
    E. Maternal behavior

25. The BEST indication of internal hemorrhaging is

    A. presence of shock
    B. pale gums
    C. blue gums
    D. blood in the urine or in the stool
    E. fainting

26. Which of the following are dominant inherited traits?

    I. A long tail
    II. A curly tail
    III. Long ears
    IV. Absence of dew claws
    V. Yellow or pearl eyes

    The CORRECT answer is:

    A. I, II, V
    B. I, II, III, V
    C. II, IV
    D. All of the above
    E. None of the above

27. One of the oldest purebreds in the world, nicknamed "the Persian Greyhound," is the

    A. Whippet
    B. Saluki
    C. Borzoi
    D. Afghan Hound
    E. Ibzian Hound

28. What breed is the SMALLEST of the working terriers? The

    A. Cairn
    B. Dandie Dinmont
    C. Bull
    D. Australian
    E. Airedale

29. The Shetland Sheepdog appears to be a *smaller* version of the

    A. Belgian Tervuren
    B. Belgian Sheepdog
    C. Belgian Malinois
    D. Rough Collie
    E. Australian Cattle Dog

30. All of the following are possible causes of Coprophagy EXCEPT

   A. boredom
   B. lack of certain digestive enzymes
   C. parasites
   D. vitamin deficiencies
   E. mineral deficiencies

31. Inflammation of the stomach lining accompanies:
   I. Salmonellosis
   II. Acute Pancreatitis
   III. Gastroenteriris
   IV. Acute Gastritis
   V. Enteritis
   The CORRECT answer is:

   A. II, III, IV, V
   B. III, IV, V
   C. III, IV
   D. I, II, IV
   E. All of the above

32. Treatment is largely dietary for:
   I. Malabsorption Syndrome
   II. Rickets
   III. Congestive Heart Failure
   IV. Liver Disease
   V. Colitis
   The CORRECT answer is:

   A. II, V
   B. II, IV, V
   C. II, III, V
   D. I, II, IV
   E. All of the above

33. Demodectic Mange occurs *mostly* in

   A. young, short-haired dogs
   B. old, long-haired dogs
   C. long-haired dogs
   D. pregnant females
   E. old, short-haired dogs

34. The castrated male
   I. will not roam
   II. will be less aggressive
   III. will stop marking territory
   IV. is more obedient to commands
   V. is more lethargic
   The CORRECT answer is:

   A. I, II, III
   B. II, IV, V
   C. I, II, III, V
   D. All of the above
   E. None of the above

35. What disease is indicated when there is stiffness of the limbs and difficult breathing?

   A. Tetanus
   B. Rabies
   C. Hypothyroidism
   D. Diabetes Inspidus
   E. Arthritis

36. Home care of breaks and fractures includes:
    I. Keeping the cast dry
    II. Giving calcium and phosphorus additives
    III. Preventing licking or chewing of the cast
    IV. Checking for evidence of increased swelling
    V. Checking for loosening of the cast
    The CORRECT answer is:

    A. I, II, III
    D. II, III, IV, V
    B. II, III, IV
    E. All of the above
    C. I, III, IV, V

36._____

37. To insure conception, repeated breeding is recommended every _____ hours.

    A. six
    D. forty-eight
    B. twelve
    E. seventy-two
    C. twenty-four

37._____

38. All of the following are grouped as fat-soluble vitamins EXCEPT

    A. A   B. B-12   C. D   D. E   E. K

38._____

39. Several factors normally assist the trailing dog. *Most important* is

    A. body odor
    B. odor left by shoes
    C. odors of crushed vegetation
    D. disturbed soil patterns
    E. visual clues in the environment

39._____

40. All of the following are true EXCEPT:

    A. Behavior traits are inherited
    B. A good environment can make a good dog of a poor puppy
    C. A bad environment can spoil a good puppy
    D. Critical periods in the life of a puppy apply equally to all breeds
    E. If socialization is neglected, the puppy is handicapped for the remainder of his life

40._____

41. Which porcupine quills should be removed FIRST? Those

    A. in the dog's mouth
    B. from behind the ribs
    C. in the dog's chest
    D. in the wrist joints
    E. on the face

41._____

42. Which breed excels at pointing game and retrieving from both land and water? The

    A. English Setter
    B. Flat-coated Retriever
    C. Chesapeake Bay Retriever
    D. Wirehaired Pointing Griffon
    E. German Short-haired Pointer

42._____

43. Formerly called the "Snap Dog," this breed resembles the Greyhound. This breed is the

    A. Italian Greyhound
    B. Whippet
    C. Miniature Pinscher
    D. Manchester Terrier
    E. Weimaraner

43._____

44. *One* of the few very large breeds that adapts well to the city and apartment life is the

    A. Mastiff
    B. Irish Wolfhound
    C. Great Dane
    D. Great Pyrenees
    E. St. Bernard

44._____

45. What breed is a member of the Mastiff Family and called "the Great Dogs of the Mountains?" The

    A. Kuvasz
    B. Great Pyrenees
    C. Bull Mastiff
    D. St. Bernard
    E. Samoyed

46. What breed is so old it is called "the companion of the pharoahs?" The

    A. Basenji
    B. Saluki
    C. Greyhound
    D. Ibzian Hound
    E. Komondor

47. When two dogs of a kind are presented together, they are called a

    A. brace
    B. couple
    C. game
    D. pack
    E. team

48. Which of the following is the *recommended* dietary procedure for adult dogs?

    A. Do not allow a dog to go without food for more than twenty-four hours
    B. Dry food should be available at all times
    C. Dogs should only be fed once a day
    D. Uneaten food should be taken away after ten minutes
    E. Dogs should not be fed within an hour of bed-time

49. All of the following should be avoided if the dog is on a low-salt diet EXCEPT

    A. commercial canned dog food
    B. dog biscuits
    C. macaroni and rice
    D. commercial dog treats
    E. table scraps

50. Dogs utilize their food more efficiently when

    A. they are fed once a day
    B. they are fed three times a day
    C. vitamins supplement the diet
    D. only dry dog is fed
    E. smaller amounts are eaten more often

KEY (CORRECT ANSWERS)

1. A	11. E	21. D	31. C	41. A
2. D	12. C	22. C	32. E	42. E
3. C	13. D	23. A	33. A	43. B
4. D	14. A	24. A	34. E	44. C
5. C	15. C	25. B	35. A	45. B
6. E	16. C	26. E	36. C	46. A
7. A	17. A	27. B	37. D	47. A
8. B	18. B	28. A	38. B	48. D
9. C	19. B	29. D	39. B	49. C
10. C	20. C	30. C	40. B	50. E

EXAMINATION SECTION

TEST 1

DIRECTIONS: Each question or incomplete statement is followed by several suggested answers or completions. Select the one that BEST answers the question or completes the statement. *PRINT THE LETTER OF THE CORRECT ANSWER IN THE SPACE AT THE RIGHT.*

1. To become accredited, a graduate veterinarian must
    A. receive approval of the State Veterinary Medical Association
    B. be licensed in the state, be a graduate of a college of veterinary medicine, pass the accreditation examination, and request accreditation by contacting state and federal animal health officials
    C. have had one year of experience since graduation
    D. hold a current license in at least two states

    1.____

2. The cooperative state-federal brucellosis eradication program is conducted
    A. under authority of state and federal laws and regulations using the recommended Uniform Methods and Rules of the USAHA as a guide
    B. under regulations of the United States Animal Health Association (USAHA)
    C. under federal regulations
    D. under state regulations

    2.____

3. The U.S. Department of Agriculture administers Public Law 89-544 (The Laboratory Animal Welfare Act) which governs the humane care and treatment of _____ used for research
    A. horses, cows, swine, rabbits, guinea pigs, and rodents
    B. all warm-blooded vertebrate animals
    C. dogs, cats, rabbits, guinea pigs, hamsters, and monkeys
    D. rabbits, rats, guinea pigs, hamsters, gerbils, and mice

    3.____

4. Which of the following is a responsibility of veterinarians conducting the tuberculin test?
    A. Consider and record all deviations from normal
    B. Require animals to be restrained when infecting tuberculin
    C. Use technical skill in application and interpretation of the test
    D. All of the above

    4.____

5. Cattle intended for export from the United States MUST
    A. be tuberculin and brucellosis tested irrespective of circumstances
    B. leave the country through the nearest port of export
    C. be vaccinated for shipping fever according to regulations
    D. be accompanied to port of embarkation by a properly issued and endorsed health certificate

    5.____

6. Amendments to the federal regulations which deal with animal disease control and eradication activities are
   A. formulated by the Association of State Department of Agriculture
   B. acted upon by Congress
   C. published in all local newspapers to meet legal requirements
   D. promulgated by the Animal Health Division, ARS, and U.S. Department of Agriculture

6.____

7. One of the stated purposes of the Laboratory Animal Welfare Act is to
   A. have government control of animals used during actual research
   B. protect owners of dogs and cats from theft of such animals
   C. prevent the unnecessary use of animals for research
   D. promote a more efficient usage of the animals covered by the Act

7.____

8. The person responsible for familiarizing the accredited veterinarian with state and federal requirements relative to hog cholera regulations for shipping swine is the
   A. accredited veterinarian himself
   B. area veterinarian
   C. president of the veterinarian's state association
   D. ANH veterinarian in charge

8.____

9. The standards as required by the Laboratory Animal Welfare Act and as developed by USDA cover
   A. maximum requirements to attain humane care and handling of the involved species of animals
   B. maximum requirements for housing, feeding, watering, sanitation, ventilation, shelter, separation of species, and veterinary care
   C. minimum requirements for housing, feeding, watering, sanitation, ventilation, shelter, separation of species, and veterinary care
   D. the development of protocol for conducting research on the involved species of animals

9.____

10. The accredited veterinarian should
    A. become well versed in his/her responsibilities to the state-federal hog cholera eradication program
    B. see that swine with hog cholera are shipped immediately for slaughter
    C. understand all phases of the state-federal hog cholera eradication program
    D. be able to carry out both A and C

10.____

11. A carload of aged female cattle is being shipped to Canada for slaughter purposes only. To satisfy our export requirements, they MUST be inspected and
    A. exported through a designated port
    B. tested negative to tuberculosis alone
    C. shipped by rail only
    D. tested negative to tuberculosis and brucellosis

11.____

12. Outbreaks of domestic and suspected foreign poultry diseases should be reported by accredited veterinarians to   12.____
    A. public health officials
    B. local news media
    C. the appropriate state or federal animal health officials
    D. county sheriff

13. Official interstate health certificates may be issued only by   13.____
    A. accredited veterinarians and livestock inspectors
    B. graduate veterinarians
    C. accredited veterinarians and state or federal employees who are veterinarians
    D. licensed veterinarians

14. When identifying cattle with eartags for any official reason, the veterinarian should   14.____
    A. place an official tag in every animal
    B. place an official tag in every animal and, in addition, record the numbers of other tags already in the animals
    C. place official tags in untagged animals and record the numbers of other tags already in the animals
    D. leave the eartags with the owner

15. Responsibility for obtaining information concerning the health requirements of the country of destination, including a prior permit, rests PRIMARILY with the   15.____
    A. accredited veterinarian   B. state official
    C. carrier   D. exporter

16. Specimens from suspected vesicular and foreign diseases should   16.____
    A. not be shipped anywhere until shipment is approved
    B. be shipped immediately to the state-federal official in the state
    C. be shipped immediately to the Plum Island Laboratory
    D. be shipped immediately to the State Diagnostic Laboratory nearest the suspected outbreak

17. The PRIMARY responsibility for the control of interstate movements of animals lies with the   17.____
    A. Animal Health Division, USDA
    B. U.S. Animal Health Association
    C. Animal Health officials of the state of destination
    D. Interstate Commerce Commission

18. The state-federal Emergency Animal Disease Eradication Organization has been established in each state to handle   18.____
    A. rabies in domestic animals
    B. investigate cases of scrapie in sheep
    C. outbreaks of exotic foreign animal diseases
    D. all livestock diseases

19. A mink breeder requests for export shipment of two breeding minks to Canada, the issuance of a health certificate by an accredited veterinarian and an endorsement of the certificate by an ANH Division veterinarian authorized to perform that service. 19.____
    A. The regulations of the Department require the issuance and endorsement of health certificates for the export shipment of mink.
    B. The accredited veterinarian cannot issue a health certificate for the export shipment of mink because there are no applicable regulations for such animals.
    C. The ANH Division has no objection to the issuance and endorsement of health certificates for the export shipment of mink if only accurate and true statements are made thereon.
    D. None of the statements is correct.

20. The use of diagnostic facilities at the National Animal Disease Laboratory, Ames, Iowa, are available 20.____
    A. to accredited veterinarians only after clearance with their veterinarian in charge of the ANH Division
    B. for the identification of certain disease organisms
    C. to accredited veterinarians with no local diagnostic facilities
    D. to all accredited veterinarians wishing to identify or confirm suspected disease conditions

21. An importer offers for entry into the United States at the Port of New York a dozen live adult partridges from Germany. These birds to be eligible for entry must be: 21.____
    I. quarantined for a specific minimum period
    II. accompanied by a prior permit from the Hyattsville office of the ANH Division
    III. accompanied by a health certificate issued by a salaried veterinarian of the German Government
    The CORRECT answer is:
    A. All three statements are correct.
    B. Only statements I and III are correct.
    C. Only statement II is correct.
    D. None of the statements are correct.

22. The responsibility of an accredited veterinarian when confronted with possible screw-worm infestations is to 22.____
    A. identify any specimens found and report the identification to state or federal authorities
    B. treat infested wounds and spray the entire herd
    C. collect specimens, treat the wound, and submit the specimens to state or federal animal disease officials for identification

23. John Doe wishes to import a prize Hereford bull directly to the United States from a country infected with foot and mouth disease, subsequent to quarantine at the Department's quarantine station at the Port of New York. He 23.____
    A. must make arrangements to quarantine of the animal for 60 days
    B. cannot do so because the movement which he proposes is presently prohibited by law
    C. must have the bull tested
    D. must first obtain a prior permit from the AND Division in Hyattsville and must see that properly completed test charts and a health certificate accompany the animal

24. The Uniform Methods and Rules for Tuberculosis Eradication are changed 24.____
    A. when found necessary by a meeting of state veterinarians
    B. locally, when a state cannot get the required number of cattle tested
    C. when infection has been reduced to the vanishing point
    D. when recommended by the United States Animal Health Association and approved by the Animal Health Division of the U.S Department of Agriculture

25. The cervical tuberculin test is used in known infected herds 25.____
    A. because it never fails to detect all of the tuberculosis infections in the herd
    B. because it is an easier place to inject
    C. because it appears more professional to the owner
    D. when directed by local/state and federal officials

26. Vesicular conditions and other animal diseases NOT readily recognized or easily diagnosed should be reported to state and federal animal health officials promptly and without fail because 26.____
    A. only domestic diseases are considered of importance
    B. it is necessary to test the efficiency of state-federal emergency disease eradication organizations
    C. increased world traffic by air and surface routes is multiplying the danger of foreign animal diseases entering the country
    D. indemnity money may be available

27. When scrapie is suspected, the MOST important procedure to follow is to 27.____
    A. recommend immediate slaughter of affected animals
    B. report it immediately to state or federal animal health officials
    C. cull and ship for slaughter
    D. treat the sheep symptomatically

28. Frozen beef from foot and mouth disease infected countries is permitted entry into the U.S. 28.____
    A. if the shipment is transported under seal
    B. if upon inspection at the port of entry the shipment is accompanied by a proper certificate
    C. if the meat is packed in substantial tight leak-proof containers
    D. all of the above are correct

29. In reporting the history of a group of sheep suspected of having scrapie to the animal health official, which factor do you consider the MOST important?
    A. Whether the sheep are managed as a range band or farm flock
    B. Prevalence of sucking insects
    C. Purchases and sales in the past three to four years
    D. Quality of feed and general sanitation

29.____

30. Beef products may be imported into the U.S. from a country where foot and mouth disease exists without restriction if
    A. effective and acceptable processing has been done in the country of origin
    B. the animals from which product is derived are vaccinated
    C. the shipment is moved directly to the port of entry
    D. the product is in tight containers

30.____

31. Anaplasmosis, an infectious and transmissible disease of cattle characterized by destruction of the erythrocytes
    A. is an example of another livestock disease that has been eradicated from the United States by the efforts of accredited veterinarians and cooperating state and federal regulatory officials
    B. has shown no response to broad-spectrum antibiotic treatment
    C. has been reported in a majority of the states and movement of infected animals is subject to state and federal restrictions
    D. has been kept out of the United States by prompt application of control measures in the Hawaiian Islands in 1955

31.____

32. What does RESTRICTED ENTRY of animal by-products mean?
    A. Inspection of cargo at dockside
    B. Supervision of handling
    C. Release only to previously approved establishments
    D. All of the above

32.____

33. Which of the following possible courses of action by an accredited veterinarian in scabies work is NOT acceptable?
    A. Treat known cases without reporting to animal health officials
    B. Acquire information relative to origin and possible spread of infestation
    C. Issue certificates for scabies-free sheep to move interstate
    D. Report all suspected cases to animal health officials

33.____

34. Before importing cultures of animal disease causing organisms, a scientist must obtain a permit from the USDA for the importation of
    A. all such cultures
    B. those organisms not present in the United States
    C. those organisms which will be used in studies involving animal inoculation
    D. those cultures originating in countries infected with foot and mouth disease or rinderpest

34.____

35. In the control and eradication of scabies in sheep or cattle, the accredited veterinarian should
    A. issue the permit for slaughter of affected sheep or cattle
    B. spray the infected animals
    C. arrange for dipping in chlordane
    D. do none of the above

35.____

KEY (CORRECT ANSWERS)

1.	B	11.	A	21.	A	31.	C
2.	A	12.	C	22.	C	32.	D
3.	C	13.	C	23.	B	33.	A
4.	D	14.	B	24.	D	34.	A
5.	D	15.	D	25.	D	35.	D
6.	D	16.	A	26.	C		
7.	B	17.	A	27.	B		
8.	A	18.	C	28.	D		
9.	C	19.	C	29.	C		
10.	D	20.	A	30.	A		

16

EXAMINATION SECTION
TEST 1

DIRECTIONS: Each question consists of a statement. You are to indicate whether the statement is TRUE (T) or FALSE (F). *PRINT THE LETTER OF THE CORRECT ANSWER IN THE SPACE AT THE RIGHT.*

1. The metenephric kidney is formed from mesodermal ducts. 1.____

2. Following birth, a long bone decreases its length by endochondial bone formation. 2.____

3. The adult tooth is formed from oral epithelium. 3.____

4. The infraorbital nerve goes through the maxillary foramen. 4.____

5. The small intestine of a pig is BEST described as a spiral colon with 5 coils. 5.____

6. Prominent features of the lungs of the horse that distinguish it from other animals include a prominent septum and NO contact between the lungs. 6.____

7. The fibula of the dog as compared to the horse is MORE developed. 7.____

8. The function of the proventriculus in the digestive system of the chicken is to secrete digestive enzymes. 8.____

9. The brain center of the autonomic nerve system is located at the hippocampus. 9.____

10. The suspensory ligament attaches to the ventral third of the last two ribs in the bitch. 10.____

11. The large artery lateral and subcutaneous in the horse's limb is the common volar digital artery. 11.____

12. The action of the gracilis muscle is extension of the hip *only*. 12.____

13. The mesenteric lymph glands are scattered throughout the mesentery. 13.____

14. In the horse, the spleen is located along the left portion of the greater curvature of the stomach. 14.____

15. The ductus arteriosis bypasses the lungs from the pulmonary artery to the aorta. 15.____

16. The syrinx is found in mammals but NOT found in birds. 16.____

17. The radial nerve provides innervation to the extensors of the foreleg. 17.____

18. The transthoracic muscle in an opened bovine carcass is cut through to examine the sternal lymph node. 18.____

19. The reciprocal apparatus in the hind limb of the horse causes the hock to flex when the stifle is extended. 19.____

20. The iliac artery is the MAIN artery to the rumen. 20.____

21. The margo plicatus separates the non-glandular (esophageal) part and the glandular (cardiac and pyline) parts of the stomach of a horse. 21.____

17

22. The deep digital flexor CANNOT move if the fetlock is held and *only* the toe is flexed.   22.____
23. The cardiac cycle of isometric contraction extends from opening of the A-V valves to closing of the semilunar valves.   23.____
24. The symphysis pelvis is the joint noted for its stability rather than motility.   24.____
25. The small colon of the horse terminates at the beginning of the rectum at the pelvic inlet.   25.____
26. In the cow and sheep, the reticulum lies between the rumen and the omasum.   26.____
27. The stomach receives blood from ALL branches of the celiac.   27.____
28. The spleen is on the right side of ALL mammals.   28.____
29. PROXIMAL is defined as remote, farthest from the center, or origin.   29.____
30. The paired cavities of the brain are the lateral ventricles of the cerebral hemispheres.   30.____
31. Blood supply of the thoracic cavity is derived *only* from the internal thoracic artery (bronchial).   31.____
32. The trochlear and hypogloseal are motor cranial nerves.   32.____
33. The excretory ducts of the kidneys are the ureters.   33.____
34. The pulmonary artery connects the heart to the brain.   34.____
35. The pharynx connects the oral cavity and nasal cavity with the esophagus and larynx.   35.____
36. Venous fluid is carried by the pulmonary artery.   36.____
37. The esophageal and tracheal twigs of the common carotid supply the esophagus.   37.____
38. The jugular vein is on the right side of the neck *only* in ALL animals.   38.____
39. In the cow, the esophagus connects the rumen and pharynx.   39.____
40. Two structures joined by the first rib include the first thoracic and last cervical vertebrae.   40.____
41. In the horse, the cecum is located *almost* entirely on the left.   41.____
42. The nerves connecting the autonomic with the somatic nerves are the inter-neurons.   42.____
43. In postural reflexes, the movements are made smooth and steady by the cerebrum.   43.____
44. The common characteristic of the colon of the cow, sheep, and pig is that it is coiled.   44.____
45. In a horse presented with radial nerve paralysis, crepitation and NO weight bearing on the affected limb is suffering from a radial bone fracture.   45.____
46. Anaplasia is the change of any adult type of tissue to another adult type of tissue.   46.____
47. The basal border of the lungs in a horse are a curved line from the costochondral junction of the 6th rib along the 8th and 9th costal cartilages to the end of the next to last intercostal space.   47.____

48. The radial nerve provides innervation to the extensors of the foreleg.   48._____

49. The olfactory nerve is the *only* sensory cranial nerve.   49._____

50. The facial nerve has a motor function *only*.   50._____

KEY (CORRECT ANSWERS)

1.	T	11.	F	21.	T	31.	F	41.	F
2.	F	12.	F	22.	F	32.	T	42.	T
3.	T	13.	T	23.	F	33.	T	43.	F
4.	T	14.	T	24.	T	34.	F	44.	T
5.	F	15.	T	25.	F	35.	T	45.	T
6.	F	16.	F	26.	T	36.	T	46.	F
7.	T	17.	T	27.	T	37.	T	47.	T
8.	T	18.	T	28.	F	38.	F	48.	T
9.	F	19.	F	29.	F	39.	T	49.	F
10.	T	20.	F	30.	T	40.	T	50.	F

TEST 2

Questions 1-20

DIRECTIONS: Answer the following questions directly, briefly, and succinctly.

1. The location of the left kidney in the dog corresponds to the bodies of which lumbar vertebrae?
2. How many cranial nerves does a cow have?
3. What does CAUDAL mean?
4. In the horse, with what organs does the esophagus connect?
5. What goes through the maxillary foramen of the pterygopalatine fossa?
6. In what species does endotheliochorial placentation occur?
7. Where is the choroid plexus found in the dog?
8. In what bone is the infraorbital conal located?
9. What are the paired glands next to the ischial arch in the bull?
10. What is the smallest unit of air exchange in the avian lung?
11. From which layer are the lung, liver, and pancreas derived during fetal development?
12. In the cow, what is the hard structure lateral and caudal to the plane of the urethral orifices?
13. Which vessel carries blood from the fetal placenta to the fetus?
14. What is the efferent branch of the patellar reflex?
15. Up to what layer of the epidermis does the blood supply go?
16. From which of the following embryonic structures is the nervous system formed?
17. What muscle is unaffected by paralysis of the facial nerve?
18. In what animal is the cecum on the left side?
19. What nerve innervates extensors of the forearm?
20. What is the location of the pituitary fossa?

Questions 21-35

DIRECTIONS: Fill in the blank space(s) the word (or words) which is (are) the correct answer(s) to the question.

21. The PREPUCE defines _____.
22. The small intestine of the horse begins at the _____.

23. The nerve that curves around the distal third of the scapula and that may be damaged by stretching is the _____. 23.____

24. The outside layer of the umbilical cord is the _____. 24.____

25. The type of placentation in ovines is _____. 25.____

26. The ureters of the chicken open into the _____. 26.____

27. The great transverse commisure connecting the two cerebral hemispheres is known as the _____. 27.____

28. The location of the deltoid tuberosity in the horse is the _____. 28.____

29. The fertilized egg splits into segments called _____. 29.____

30. The cornual nerve is a branch of the _____. 30.____

31. The gracilis muscle acts to _____. 31.____

32. The umbilical vein of the fetus becomes the _____. 32.____

33. The peroneal nerve lies between the _____. 33.____

34. Femoral head and neck abnormalities characterized by an *increase* in the angle between the femoral neck and shaft is called _____. 34.____

35. The scratch reflex is mediated in the _____. 35.____

KEY (CORRECT ANSWERS)

1. 2nd, 3rd, and 4th.
2. 12.
3. Tail shaped, or toward the tail or posterior extremity.
4. Stomach and pharynx.
5. The infraorbital nerve and vessels.
6. Dog and cat.
7. 4th ventricle brain.
8. Maxilla.
9. Bulbourethral.
10. The air capillaries.
11. Entoderm.
12. Major vestibular gland.
13. Umbilical vein.
14. The femoral nerve.
15. Stratus germinatium.
16. The ectoderm.
17. Levator palpebrae (eyelid)
18. The pig.
19. Radial.
20. Central portion of sphenoid bone.
21. the fold of skin covering the glands penis when not erect (foreskin or sheath)
22. pyloris of the stomach
23. suprascapular
24. endoderm of the amnion
25. cotyledonary
26. urodenum
27. corpus collosum
28. left shaft of the humerus
29. blastomeres
30. trigeminal nerve
31. adduct the limb
32. ligamentum teres hepaticum
33. long digital extensor and lateral digital extensor
34. coxa vulga
35. spinal cord

EXAMINATION SECTION
TEST 1

DIRECTIONS: Each question or incomplete statement is followed by several suggested answers or completions. Select the one that BEST answers the question or completes the statement. *PRINT THE LETTER OF THE CORRECT ANSWER IN THE SPACE AT THE RIGHT.*

1. The muscle of mastication affected by facial paralysis is the   1.____
   - A. genioglossus
   - B. buccinator
   - C. massater
   - D. pterygoideus

2. The bones making up the hard palate in MOST animals are   2.____
   - A. malar
   - B. maxillae
   - C. sphenoid
   - D. temporalis

3. The maxillary sinus of the bovine communicates *directly* with the   3.____
   - A. frontal sinus
   - B. palantine
   - C. pharynx
   - D. cornual diverticulum

4. Gastric mucosa is composed of _____ cells.   4.____
   - A. columnar
   - B. stratified columnar
   - C. squamous
   - D. transitional

5. The horse's age is judged by eruption of teeth.   5.____
   When the intermediate incisors are erupted, the horse is _____ years old.
   - A. 2 1/2
   - B. 3 1/2
   - C. 4 1/2
   - D. 5

6. The suspensory ligament of the ovary runs into the   6.____
   - A. thoracic part of the abdomen
   - B. near tuber coxae
   - C. oviduct
   - D. uterus

7. A radiograph shows a fracture of the tibial tuberosity. Which of the following are involved?   7.____
   - A. Extensors of the stifle
   - B. Flexors of the stifle
   - C. Extensors of the hip
   - D. Flexors of the hip

8. The muscle running cranioventral on the lateral abdominal wall is the   8.____
   - A. rectus abdomenous
   - B. internal oblique
   - C. external oblique
   - D. transverse abdomenous

9. The muscle(s) tensed when the anterior portion of the 3rd phalanx is lifted is (are) the   9.____
   - A. suspensory ligament
   - B. suspensory ligament and deep digital flexor
   - C. superficial flexor
   - D. long digital extensor

10. The structure with the LEAST sensitivity to radiation is the

    A. hemopoietic system
    B. skeletal system
    C. nervous system
    D. skin

11. The efferent lymphatics of the tunica vaginalis of the bull drain into the _____ lymph node.

    A. deep inguinal
    B. superficial
    C. popliteal
    D. femoral

12. The action of the gracilis muscle is to

    A. extend the stifle joint
    B. abduct the front limb
    C. flex the stifle joint
    D. adduct the hind limb

13. What is the main factor in the maintenance of negative intrathoracic pressure?

    A. Closure of the glottis after inspection
    B. Dilation of the bronchi
    C. Contraction of the diaphragm
    D. Pressure of abdominal organs on the diaphragm

14. The spinal nerves originate from the

    A. neural crest
    B. mantle of neural tube
    C. ependymal cells
    D. neuroglia

15. A nail entering the sole at the apex of the front and extending upwards toward the distal phalangeal articulation will pass through the

    A. deep digital flexor
    B. superficial digital flexor
    C. coronary band
    D. periople

16. The cerebro-spinal fluid from the ventricles communicates with that of the subarachroid space by the

    A. foramen of monro
    B. central canal of the spinal cord
    C. foramen of magendie
    D. foramen magnum

17. What organs does the celiac artery of the dog supply?

    A. Stomach, liver, spleen, pancreas and 1st part of duodenum
    B. Stomach, spleen, pancreas
    C. Liver, spleen, 1st part of duodenum
    D. Stomach, liver, pancreas and 1st part of duodenum

18. Which of the following nerve tracts are descending?

    A. Rubrospinal
    B. Tectospinal
    C. Cerebrospinal
    D. ALL of the above

19. A jugular vein puncture in the upper 1/2 of the neck occurs because the jugular is separated from the carotid by the

    A. sterno cephalicus
    B. omohyoideus
    C. sternothyrodeus
    D. brachialis

20. In what structure in the intestine does the integrity of an intestinal suture lie?

    A. Muscularis
    B. Mucosa
    C. Submucosa
    D. Serosa

21. The vessel which carries oxygenated blood to the fetus is the

    A. hepatic artery
    B. hepatic vein
    C. umbilical artery
    D. umbilical vein

22. The lymphatics of the tunica vaginalis of the bull's penis drain to the _____ lymph node.

    A. deep inguinal
    B. superficial inguinal
    C. prefemoral
    D. superficial iliac

23. Which muscle suspends the trunk of the animal between the shoulder blades?

    A. Cranial pectoral
    B. Caudal pectoral
    C. Trapezius
    D. Serratus Ventralis

24. The efferent lymphatics from the tunica vaginalis of the bull drain into the iliac node. Where do carotid arteries branch from?

    A. Right brachial
    B. Left brachial
    C. Brachrocephalic

25. The central vein of a hepatic lobule

    A. bypasses the sinusoids
    B. is going to the sinusoids
    C. has come from the sinusoids
    D. comes from the portal vein

KEY (CORRECT ANSWERS)

1.	B	11.	A
2.	B	12.	D
3.	B	13.	C
4.	A	14.	A
5.	B	15.	A
6.	A	16.	C
7.	A	17.	A
8.	B	18.	D
9.	D	19.	A
10.	C	20.	C

21. D
22. A
23. D
24. C
25. C

TEST 2

DIRECTIONS: Each question or incomplete statement is followed by several suggested answers or completions. Select the one that BEST answers the question or completes the statement. *PRINT THE LETTER OF THE CORRECT ANSWER IN THE SPACE AT THE RIGHT.*

1. The distal patellar ligaments of the horse are 1.____

    A. three strong bands connecting the patella with the tibial tuberosity
    B. two strong bands attaching the patella to the epicondyles of the femur
    C. three strong bands attaching the patella to the tendon of the quadriceps
    D. three strong bands attaching the patella to the neck of the femur

2. The action of the gracilis muscle is to 2.____

    A. abduct the rear leg
    B. extend the stifle
    C. adduct the limb
    D. flex the rear leg

3. What is true of the normal anatomy of the newborn calf? 3.____

    A. Esophageal groove in rudimentary
    B. Rumen and reticulum = 1/2 abomasum
    C. Reticulum and omosum = abomasum
    D. Rumen and reticulum = abomasum

4. Unilateral paralysis of lips indicates damage to the _____ nerve. 4.____

    A. trigeninal   B. masseter
    C. facial   D. lingual

5. In the dog, where does the cranial cruciate ligament run? 5.____

    A. Cranio-medial surface of the lateral condyle of the femur to the posterior tibia
    B. Caudo-medial of the lateral condyle of the femur to the anterior tibia
    C. Caudo-lateral of the medial condyle of the humerus to the anterior tibia
    D. Caudo-lateral tibia to the cranio-medial femur

6. The external spermatic artery branches from the 6.____

    A. abdominal aorta
    B. circumflex iliac artery
    C. external iliac
    D. internal iliac

7. The renal blood supply 7.____

    A. mostly bypasses the glometulus
    B. serves the distal convoluted tubules before reaching the glomerulus
    C. serves the glomerulus before the rest of the kidney
    D. is evenly distributed throughout the kidney

8. Esophageal stenosis due to a vascular ring at the base of the heart is due to

    A. *right* displacement of the heart in the thorax
    B. a persistent 4th aortic arch with *right* ductus arteriosis
    C. a persistent 4th *left* aortic arch with *left* ductus arteriosis
    D. a persistent 4th *right* aortic arch with *left* ductus arteriosis

9. The muscle attaching to the brim of the pelvis and prepubic tendon, caudal to the external inguinal ring, is the

    A. iliopeas   B. pectineus
    C. obturator   D. gluteal

10. The cerebro-spinal fluid from the ventricles communicates with that of the subarachroid space by the

    A. foramen of monro
    B. central canal of the spinal cord
    C. foramen of magendie
    D. foramen magnum

11. Two species without gallbladders are the

    A. horse and mouse   B. horse and rat
    C. horse and rabbit   D. guinea pig and mouse

12. The parasympathetic nerve supply to the rectum is via the

    A. hypogastric nerves   B. lumbar splanchnic nerves
    C. pudendal nerve   D. pelvic nerves

13. The nerve to the flexor carpi radialis is the

    A. lateral femoropatellar   B. lateral collateral
    C. medial collateral   D. medial patellar

14. The muscle most important in normal respiration is the

    A. scalenus   B. internal intercostals
    C. external intercostals   D. diaphragm

15. Hyperplasia of the parathyroid gland is caused by

    A. chronic interstitial nephritis   B. chronic interstitial hepatitis
    C. diet   D. chronic enteritis

16. Goitrogens work by

    A. stimulation of the thyroid gland
    B. stimulation of the pituitary gland
    C. stimulation of the pituitary, thyroid, and adrenal glands
    D. *decreased* thyroxin resulting in *increased* TSH

17. Acute pericarditis can cause which sequella MOST frequently? 17.____

    A. Aortic stenosis
    C. Hydropericardium
    B. Fibrinous pericarditis
    D. Mural thrombosis

18. Clinically, a sertoli cell tumor exhibits 18.____

    A. virilism
    C. feminization
    B. polyuria
    D. no signs

19. Os rostralis is found in 19.____

    A. dogs   B. horses   C. swine   D. cows

20. The quantity of oxygen with which 1 gm of the HB can combine is 20.____

    A. 1.0 ml   B. 1.3 ml   C. 2.3 ml   D. 5.4 ml

21. What artery is available for the pulse on a horse? 21.____

    A. Internal maxillary artery
    B. External maxillary artery
    C. Transverse facial artery
    D. Internal facial artery

22. What are the fibers found in the corpus callosum? 22.____

    A. Long association
    C. Corticothalamic
    B. Short association
    D. Commissurae

23. The end of the nephron includes the 23.____

    A. distal convoluted tubule
    B. straight collecting duct
    C. arched collecting duct
    D. minor calyx

24. A unipyramial kidney is contained in the _____ and the _____. 24.____

    A. horse, ox
    C. horse, mouse
    B. ox, sheep
    D. dog, cat

25. Which of the following is NOT considered a bone making up the Calvarium? 25.____

    A. Parietal
    C. Occipital
    B. Sphenoid
    D. Maxillary

KEY (CORRECT ANSWERS)

1.	A		11.	B
2.	C		12.	C
3.	B		13.	C
4.	C		14.	B
5.	B		15.	A
6.	A		16.	A
7.	C		17.	B
8.	D		18.	C
9.	B		19.	C
10.	C		20.	B

21. B
22. D
23. A
24. D
25. D

EXAMINATION SECTION
TEST 1

DIRECTIONS: Each question consists of a statement. You are to indicate whether the statement is TRUE (T) or FALSE (F). *PRINT THE LETTER OF THE CORRECT ANSWER IN THE SPACE AT THE RIGHT.*

1. In normal function, the kidney conserves fixed base by exchanging NH_4 for Na in Na salts in the tubules. 1.____

2. The formula from which the stroke volume of the heart is calculated is the minute volume divided by the pulse rate per minute. 2.____

3. The circulation time of the blood can be circulated by dividing the minute blood volume by the total blood volume. 3.____

4. Renin produced by an ischemic kidney is responsible for vasodilation of kidney arteries. 4.____

5. The renal threshold of a compound is the level of that compound at which large quantities of the compound are excreted. 5.____

6. Protective mechanisms of the digestive tract to protect against proteolytic enzymes is protective mucous secreted by cells. 6.____

7. Stimulation of the peripheral end of the cervical vagus in ruminants results in *decreased* intestinal motility. 7.____

8. The *primary* function of pig allantois is to release urinary wastes. 8.____

9. Aldosterone secretion by the adrenal cortex results in *decreased* sodium resorption. 9.____

10. In the blood vascular circuit, the capillary bed is the part of the vascular tree with the *total* GREATEST cross-sectional area. 10.____

11. The GREATEST sensitivity of O_2 change in the blood is reflected with aortic and carotid bodies. 11.____

12. The neuroregulatory system on the gastrointestinal tract functions to insure the orderly sequence of digestion. 12.____

13. ADH is secreted by the pituitary and had its action in urine formation by sodium retention. 13.____

14. K+ is the *only* electrolyte that can stimulate cardiac muscle. 14.____

15. The *primary* function of the posterior pituitary is storage and release of hypothalamic secretions. 15.____

16. In bovine, the *minimum* level of Hb/100 cc. of blood consistent with health is generally accepted as 8 grams/100 ml. 16.____

17. The glomerular filtration rate depends on the effective hydrostatic pressure in the glomerulus. 17.____

18. The position of the descending colon is in the right dorsal abdomen. 18.____

19. Vomition in domestic animals indicated gastric dilatation *only*.

20. A *decreased* renal glomerular filtration rate is due to a *rise* in afferent arterial pressure.

21. The first step in activation in muscle contraction is release of calcium ions in the myofibril into the sarcoplasm.

22. Hexose sugars are absorbed from the small intestine into the portal venous system as monosaccharides directly.

23. NH_4Cl is used in alkalosis problems because it acidifies.

24. The normal temperature, pulse, and respiration rate of the canine are 99.7-100, 32-44, and 8-16, respectively.

25. LH causes development of the corpus luteum and ovulation.

26. Blood is mixed with H_2SO_4, heated, and mixed with copper to give a blue color in order to test for protein.

27. The reaction of the rumen contents is just on the basic side of neutrality.

28. The basic reaction for the metabolism of glucose in the animal body is $C_6H_{12}O_6 + 6O_2 \rightarrow 6CO_2 + H_2O +$ energy.

29. Anaphylaxis results from antibody-antigen reaction in or on the tissue.

30. The cause of sinus arrhythmia in the dog is intermittent vagal stimulation associated with inspiration and expiration, usually found in a normal, quiet dog.

31. The nephron cleans waste products from the blood by removal of these products by active transport.

32. Insulin does NOT cause hypoglycemia.

33. The MOST abundant protein in the blood plasma is albumin.

34. The HIGHEST concentration of Na+ ions is in the extracellular fluid.

35. The postsynaptic membrane is stimulated by the release of ion transport.

KEY (CORRECT ANSWERS)

1.	T	16.	T
2.	T	17.	T
3.	F	18.	F
4.	F	19.	F
5.	T	20.	F
6.	T	21.	F
7.	F	22.	T
8.	F	23.	T
9.	F	24.	F
10.	T	25.	T
11.	T	26.	F
12.	T	27.	F
13.	F	28.	T
14.	F	29.	T
15.	T	30.	T

31. F
32. F
33. T
34. T
35. F

TEST 2

DIRECTIONS: Each question consists of a statement. You are to indicate whether the statement is TRUE (T) or FALSE (F). *PRINT THE LETTER OF THE CORRECT ANSWER IN THE SPACE AT THE RIGHT.*

1. In the ruminant, stimulation of the distal vagus nerve results in closure of the relaxed esophageal groove and in marked motility of rumen.   1._____

2. The horse has the *slowest* normal sedimentation rate.   2._____

3. When oxygen comes in contact with blood in the lung, it complies with hemoglobin.   3._____

4. When O_2 enters the lung, it is exchanged with CO_2.   4._____

5. Ruminal mobility starts in the reticulum.   5._____

6. The ductus arteriosus shunts blood from the pulmonary artery to the aorta in the fetus.   6._____

7. During exercise, cardiac output *increases* due to partial anoxia.   7._____

8. A skeletal motor unit is composed of the muscle, its associated nerves and blood vessels, and the bones it is attached to.   8._____

9. Estrogen is the *only* hormone produced by the ovary.   9._____

10. Recruitment defines the activation of more motor units.   10._____

11. Rheumatoid arthritis is NOT an acquired immunity defect.   11._____

12. Active transfer is transfer in which the new host picks up the parasite itself, or in which the parasite is carried to the host by a vector.   12._____

13. The cow and horse do NOT vomit.   13._____

14. Formation of acid urine in a sheep with gluconeogenesis would occur because of excess caloric intake.   14._____

15. The intestinal absorption of iron depends on the availability of organic chelating agents in digestive mucosa.   15._____

16. As body heat *increases,* the secretion of thyroxin *decreases* because the hypothalamus becomes bathed in blood.   16._____

17. The center of motor activity of sheep and goats is the midbrain at the level of the red nucleus.   17._____

18. Hypoglycemia helps cause hunger contractions.   18._____

19. Carbonicanhydrase inhibitors *increase* renal tubular reabsorption.   19._____

20. The development of calves' stomach mucosa is governed by roughage feeding.   20._____

21. The GREATEST respiratory stimulation is caused by CO_2.   21._____

22. Bilirubinemia is indicative of hemolytic anemia.

23. Taurocholic acid is found in bile.

24. The difference between white and dark muscle is the amount of myoglobin contained in the cell.

25. The respirator quotient is O_2 absorbed divided by CO_2 expired.

26. The ability of nervous impulses to travel in one direction is the result of the nodes of Ranvier.

27. The cause of hyperplasia of the parathyroid with chronic renal disease is inability to excrete phosphates.

28. The normal temperature of a cow is 100.4-103.1.

29. The blood picture after 4-8 hours of moderate stress shows neutrophila.

30. Excess urobolinogen in the urine indicates obstruction of bile ducts.

31. Turbidity in urine that disappears with the addition of acid is probably due to precipitation of $CaPO_4$.

32. With respect to contraction time, relaxation time, and refractory time, smooth muscle times are *shorter* than skeletal muscle times.

33. If the parathyroid is removed, blood calcium *decreases* and the animal dies in tetany.

34. The buffer system found in the kidney which is NOT found in the blood is $NH_3 + H^+ = NH_4^+$.

35. Blood is bright red in cyanide poisoning because it is prevented from losing O_2 to the tissues.

KEY (CORRECT ANSWERS)

1.	T		16.	T
2.	F		17.	T
3.	T		18.	T
4.	T		19.	F
5.	T		20.	T
6.	T		21.	T
7.	T		22.	F
8.	F		23.	T
9.	F		24.	F
10.	T		25.	F
11.	F		26.	F
12.	F		27.	T
13.	T		28.	T
14.	F		29.	T
15.	F		30.	F

31. T
32. F
33. T
34. T
35. T

TEST 3

Questions 1-21

DIRECTIONS: Fill in the blank space(s) the word (or words) which is (are) the correct answer(s) to the question.

1. The fraction of blood where antibodies are found is _____. 1.____
2. The MOST important factor believed to produce the force of the regurgitation process in cattle is _____. 2.____
3. In the development of the embryo, the coelom becomes the _____. 3.____
4. Secretin is formed in the small intestine where it is absorbed. Upon reaching the pancreas, it stimulates pancreatic juice. Secretin is _____. 4.____
5. Muscle pulling against immovable ojects is called _____. 5.____
6. The *primary* cause of metabolic acidosis is _____. 6.____
7. METHEMOGLOBIN is _____. 7.____
8. When oxygen enters the blood at the lung, Fe is _____. 8.____
9. Anoxia hypoxia is due to _____. 9.____
10. Na lactate is used in acidosis problems because it functions to _____. 10.____
11. The neurons of the pregaglionic sympathetic nervous system are in the _____. 11.____
12. High arterio-venous oxygen difference of the kidney indicates _____. 12.____
13. Oxygen is carried between the mother and fetus via the _____. 13.____
14. The site of RBC manufacture is _____. 14.____
15. The enzyme that activates the pancreas or digestion is _____. 15.____
16. In dogs, the vitamin rendered unabsorbable or unusable when raw egg white is fed is _____. 16.____
17. The action of heparin is quickly terminated by _____. 17.____
18. The rumen-reticulum contraction cycle begins in the _____. 18.____
19. The peak rate of pressure change in the ventricle during contraction is a measure of _____. 19.____
20. The organ that removes waste products from blood by filtrating plasma is the _____. 20.____
21. The posterior chamber of the eye is between the iris and _____. 21.____

Questions 22-35

DIRECTIONS: Answer the following questions directly, briefly and succinctly.

22. During what phase of the cardiac cycle is the coronary blood flow the HIGHEST?

23. What two cations are *principally* involved in the conduction of nerve impulses?

24. What action does antidiuretic hormone have on the kidney?

25. What is the mechanism of the action of heparin?

26. A muscle group contracts due to acetylcholine. What is necessary for subsequent coordinated contractions?

27. Where do plasma cells produce globulins?

28. What is the product of the ornithine cycle?

29. From which embryonic layer are the mammary glands formed?

30. Androgens are secreted by the testicle. Where else in the animal body are they secreted?

31. When transfer is due to an active effort on the part of the parasite, with emphasis on the invasion of the new host, what kind of transfer is taking place?

32. In what part of the brain is the respiratory center located?

33. What is the ratio of energy from fat, protein, and carbohydrates, respectively?

34. What electrolyte solution is BEST used for its acid properties?

35. At what pH, approximately, does pepsin have its optimal effect on protein breakdown?

KEY (CORRECT ANSWERS)

1. gamma globulin
2. negative pressure gradient in the esophagus
3. body cavity
4. hormone
5. isometric contraction
6. deficient bicarbonate
7. oxidized hemoglobin
8. oxidized
9. *decreased* O_2 delivered to tissue
10. alkalinize
11. thoracic lumbar spinal cord
12. high vascularity
13. umbilical artery and vein
14. bone marrow
15. secretin
16. biotin
17. protamine
18. reticulum
19. ventricular contractibility
20. kidney
21. lens
22. Diastole.
23. Na^+ and K^+
24. Reabsorption of H_2O.
25. It interferes with thrombin.
26. Acetyl cholinesterase.
27. Ribosomes and reticulum.
28. Urea.
29. Ectoderm.
30. Adrenal cortex.
31. Active transfer.
32. Upper part of pons.
33. 9:4:4
34. NH_4Cl.
35. Highly acidic

EXAMINATION SECTION
TEST 1

DIRECTIONS: Each question or incomplete statement is followed by several suggested answers or completions. Select the one that BEST answers the question or completes the statement. *PRINT THE LETTER OF THE CORRECT ANSWER IN THE SPACE AT THE RIGHT.*

1. The molecular weight of chloride is 35.5.
   A plasma with a chloride concentration of 3.55 mg/100 ml. contains

   A. 1 milliequivalent of chloride per liter
   B. 10 milliequivalent of chloride per liter
   C. 100 milliequivalent of chloride per liter
   D. 1 equivalent of chloride per liter
   E. 10 equivalent of chloride per liter

   1.____

2. The air remaining in the lungs even *after* the MOST forceful expiration, is referred to as the

   A. tidal volume
   B. inspiratory reserve volume
   C. functional residual capacity
   D. residual volume
   E. expiratory reserve volume

   2.____

3. The *known* hormones of the anterior pituitary are

   A. steroid in nature, and are not antigenic, regardless of species differences
   B. protein in nature, exhibit species differences, and may be antigenic
   C. steroid in nature, and may be antigenic because of species differences
   D. protein in nature, identical in all species, and not antigenic
   E. protein in nature, differ among species, and are not antigenic

   3.____

4. The kidney aids in keeping the composition of blood plasma constant by the

   A. elimination of plasma protein
   B. secretion of antidiuretic hormones
   C. elimination of inorganic salts
   D. inhibition of the synthesis of ammonia
   E. selective filtration of erythrocytes

   4.____

5. The kidney filtration rate is regulated primarily by the

   A. quantity of plasma electrolytes
   B. capillary pressure in the glomerulus
   C. plasma colloidal osmotic pressure
   D. osmoreceptors in the midbrain
   E. pressure changes in Bowman's capsule

   5.____

6. The filtration rate of the glomerulus is *decreased* by

   A. an *increase* in the extracellular fluid volume
   B. a *decrease* in the pressure of Bowman's capsule

   6.____

C. a *decrease* in plasma osmotic pressure
D. an *increase* in systemic blood pressure
E. constriction of the afferent arterioles

7. Aldosterone release will cause a *decrease* in the

    A. plasma chloride level
    B. amount of potassium excreted
    C. fluid volume of the body
    D. systemic blood pressure
    E. amount of sodium lost in the urine

8. When the antidiuretic hormone is secreted into the blood stream, it causes

    A. *increased* sodium reabsorption
    B. *increased* electrolyte reabsorption in the proximal tubules
    C. alterations in aldosterone levels
    D. *increased* water reabsorption from the distal tubules
    E. *decreased* extracellular fluid volume

9. The contraction of a skeletal muscle requires a quick release of energy derived from the

    A. hydrolysis of adenosine triphosphate
    B. aerobic glycolysis of glucose
    C. oxidation of lactic acid
    D. formation of glycogen
    E. mediation of pyruvic acid

10. The movement of a bolus of food down the esophagus is the result of

    A. contractions stimulated by the sight and smell of food
    B. a parasympathetic reflex excited by chewing
    C. a stimulus in the upper part of the esophagus due to the act of swallowing
    D. a pressure gradient created by the piston-like action of the tongue during swallowing
    E. facilitation by the cephalic phase of gastric activity

11. In renal epithelium, the cells with a brush border and a cytoplasm staining eosinophilic, are found in the

    A. nephron
    B. distal convoluted tubules
    C. glomerulus
    D. proximal convoluted tubules
    E. collecting ducts

12. Antibodies are modified gammaglobulin which is formed *primarily* in the

    A. liver cells   B. spleen cells   C. R-E cells
    D. plasma cells   E. monocytes

13. The absorption of glucose in the small intestine is

    A. retarded *greatly* during insulin deficiencies
    B. dependent upon adequate bile salt secretion by the liver

C. *largely* a process of diffusion across the mucous membrane
D. accomplished by an active transport mechanism
E. MORE rapid than the absorption of galactose

14. Sinus arrythemia in the dog is caused by an *increase*

   A. in serum cholesterol
   B. and *decrease* in serum HCO_3
   C. and *decrease* in vagal tone
   D. and *decrease* in sympathetic activity
   E. and *decrease* in the activity of the strial node

15. Which of the following statements referring to the digestive system in animals is *correct*?

   A. In carnivores the intestinal villi extend the full length of the digestive tract. In other species, they are present *only* in the small intestine
   B. The pars intestinalis of the common bile duct perforates the intestinal wall at an angle. Goblet cells are present in the epithelium of the sheep, dog, cat, but are absent in other species
   C. The muscular tunic of the intestine consists of an inner circular layer and an outer longitudinal layer, which in carnivores forms taeniae
   D. Taste buds are very sparse in the fungiform papillae of carnivores but are numerous in cattle and horses
   E. The glandular stomach of carnivores exhibits a stratum compactum which lies adjacent to the muscularis mucosae

16. The energy obtained by the micro-organisms of the rumen through cellulose fermentation may be used to

   A. promote their intracellular protein synthesis
   B. promote their utilization of short-chain fatty acids
   C. provide the ruminant animal with an immediate source of energy for muscular contraction
   D. convert cellulose to intraruminal glucose
   E. promote ruminal motility

17. A hormonal secretion of the small intestinal mucosa that results in a pancreatic secretion rich in digestive enzymes is

   A. entergostrone   B. pancreatin   C. pancreozymin
   D. enterocrinin   E. secretin

18. Fragility is used in testing the resistance of RBC's by suspending them for a given time in varying dilutions of

   A. HOH   B. NaOH   C. NaCl   D. $NaHCO_3$ E. HCl

19. In normal blood, the clot begins to retract in a test tube within

   A. 1 hr.   B. 4 hrs.   C. 12 hrs.   D. 6 hrs.   E. 24 hrs.

20. The *usual* dilution when performing an erythrocyte count is

   A. 1:20   B. 1:80   C. 1:100   D. 1:150   E. 1:200

21. According to several authors, the MOST important function of the osteoclast is to 21.____

    A. store calcium and phosphorus
    B. phagocytize foreign material
    C. dissolve bone
    D. calcify cartilage
    E. produce osteoid

22. When skeletal muscle pulls against an immovable object, the type of contraction shown 22.____
    by that muscle is called

    A. isomolar   B. isometric   C. isotonic
    D. isopotential   E. isolateral

23. Regurgitation in a ruminant commences with 23.____

    A. *increased* ruminal pressure
    B. inspiration on a closed glottis
    C. *increased* omasal activity
    D. *increased* rectal pressure
    E. stimulation of the vomiting center

24. The partial pressures of oxygen, expressed in mm of mercury, at the arterial and at the 24.____
    venous ends of the pulmonary capillaries are, respectively,

    A. 40 and 50   B. 40 and 104   C. 47 and 206
    D. 47 and 567   E. 104 and 40

25. The body fluid that is *highest* in protein is 25.____

    A. urine   B. lymph   C. chyle   D. plasma   E. serum

KEY (CORRECT ANSWERS)

1.	A		11.	D
2.	D		12.	D
3.	B		13.	D
4.	C		14.	C
5.	B		15.	E
6.	E		16.	A
7.	E		17.	C
8.	D		18.	C
9.	A		19.	A
10.	C		20.	E

21. C
22. B
23. B
24. B
25. D

TEST 2

DIRECTIONS: Each question or incomplete statement is followed by several suggested answers or completions. Select the one that BEST answers the question or completes the statement. *PRINT THE LETTER OF THE CORRECT ANSWER IN THE SPACE AT THE RIGHT.*

1. Biochemical mediators of acute inflammation include 1.____

    A. plasmin and fibrinogen
    B. norepinephrine and kinekrein
    C. histadine and epinephrine
    D. histamine and bradykinin
    E. hysozyme and leukotoxin

2. The cardiac output, expressed in ml/min, is obtained by dividing the 2.____

    A. arteriovenous oxygen difference (ml/ml of blood) by the pulse rate per minute
    B. arteriovenous oxygen difference (ml/ml of blood) by the stroke volume in ml and multiplying by the pulse rate per minute
    C. oxygen absorbed per minute by the lungs (ml/min) by the stroke volume in ml
    D. oxygen absorbed per minute by the lungs (ml/min) by the arteriovenous oxygen difference (ml/ml of blood)
    E. arteriovenous oxygen difference (ml/ml of blood) by the oxygen absorbed per minute by the lungs (ml/min)

3. A clinical laboratory worker has inadvertently mislabeled three samples of citrated whole blood; one taken from a horse, one from a cow, and one from a dog. He plans to distinguish between the samples by observing the sedimentation rate of each one. 3.____
The order in which sedimentation of the blood cells of the samples will occur from the most rapid to the least rapid is:

    A. Horse, cow, dog   B. Dog, cow, horse
    C. Cow, dog, horse   D. Horse, dog, cow
    E. Cow, horse, dog

4. When glucose is to be determined, sodium fluoride is added to a blood sample because it 4.____

    A. inhibits glycolysis produced by enzymes in the erythrocytes
    B. ties up non-glucose-reducing substances which interfere
    C. facilitates the precipitation of proteins by the somogyi procedure
    D. prevents the release of thromboplastic substance and factor VII
    E. adjusts the pH to prevent oxidation in transit

5. The pH of the phosphate buffer used in Wright's stain is 5.____

    A. 6.4   B. 7.2   C. 5.0   D. 2.4   E. 5.8

6. In the normal dog, the blood cells that constitute the *largest* percentage of the leukocytes are the 6.____

    A. monocytes   B. basophils   C. neutrophils
    D. lymphocytes   E. eosinophils

7. A urine sample collected from a dog following an 18-hour water fast would indicate the MOST complete renal insufficiency if its specific gravity were

   A. 1.005   B. 1.010   C. 1.015   D. 1.020   E. 1.025

8. Blood vessels are *usually* absent from _____ tissue.

   A. muscle   B. nerve   C. connective
   D. epithelial   E. bone

9. Which of the following factors DOES NOT enter into the clotting process?

   A. Thromboplastin   B. Prothrombin   C. Antithrombin
   D. Fibrinogen   E. Sodium salts

10. There is considerable evidence that, in the case of skeletal muscle, neuromuscular transmission is mediated by acetylcholine, which is considered by many authorities to cause

    A. an *increase* in motor end-plate membrane potential
    B. an *increase* in motor end-plate membrane permeability
    C. repolarization of the motor end-plate membrane
    D. destruction of the enzyme choline-acetylase
    E. destruction of the enzyme acetylochlinesterase

11. What is the cause of the normal venous pulse in the cow?

    A. Bulging of the right a-v valve into the atrium
    B. The volume of the atrium being larger than the ventricle
    C. Contraction of the atrium
    D. Insufficiency of the right a-v valve
    E. Stenosis

12. The fluid in hepatic sinusoids is

    A. chyle   B. lymph   C. chyme   D. bile   E. blood

13. On an electrocardiogram, the interval describing the rest period for the atria is the

    A. Ta-P   B. Q-P   C. S-T   D. Tv-P   E. P-T

14. The deamination of amino acids with the formation of urea occurs in the liver of the dog. The chemical scheme defining the formation of urea is knowa as the

    A. ornithine, citrulline cycle
    B. tricarboxylic acid cycle
    C. Knoop's beta oxidation theory
    D. Krebs cycle
    E. citric acid cycle

15. The approximate amount of energy in calories in each gram of the three major foodstuffs is:

	CARBOHYDRATE	FAT	PROTEIN
A.	9	4	4
B.	4	9	4
C.	4	4	9
D.	6	8	4
E.	8	6	4

16. A compound that has an acidifying effect on the animal body is

   A. sodium acetate   B. sodium propionate
   C. sodium chloride   D. ammonium chloride
   E. ammonium citrate

17. The percentage of iron in the hemoglobin molecule is

   A. 0.34%   B. 0.49%   C. 0.68%   D. 0.94%   E. 1.23%

18. For a dog, the normal blood urea nitrogen content in mg/100 ml is

   A. 1 - 3   B. 10 - 20   C. 50 - 75
   D. 100 - 120   E. 300 - 350

19. Vitamin C deficiency may be induced in domestic animals that synthesize vitamin C by feeding them an excess of

   A. tyrosine   B. calcium   C. glucose
   D. histidine   E. riboflavin

20. Somatic sensory neurons synapse

   A. at the terminal arborizations of the axon
   B. in the dorsal root ganglia
   C. at the nodes of Ranvier
   D. in the spinal cord
   E. in ganglia of the sympathetic chain

21. The respiratory quotient for glucose metabolism is

   A. 0.10   B. 0.60   C. 0.83   D. 1.00   E. 6.00

22. Water is absorbed from gut contents in *greatest* quantity from the

   A. colon   B. small intestine   C. rectum
   D. stomach   E. cecum

23. Name the functions of the liver:

   A. Store carbohydrates as glycogen
   B. Regulate blood glucose (source of body heat)
   C. Form fatty acids from CHO and proteins (glyconeogenesis)
   D. Desaturate the saturated fats
   E. All of the above

24. Which of the following is an *essential* amino acid?

    A. Leucine	B. Methionine	C. Cystine
    D. Norleucine	E. Tyrosine

25. The PO_2 of pulmonary venous blood is approximately

    A. 25 mm. hg.	B. 40 mm. hg.	C. 65 mm. hg.
    D. 80 mm. hg.	E. 95 mm. hg.

26. The action of vitamin K involves

    A. prothrombin to thrombin
    B. fibrin to fibrinogen
    C. the production of prothrombin by the liver
    D. the production of fibrin
    E. increasing the stability of platelets

27. The combining of O_2, H_2O and CO_2 in the cell to produce needed energy is called

    A. assimilation	B. respiration	C. osmosis
    D. reproduction	E. metabolism

28. The amount of concentrated HCl, in ml., needed to make 1 liter of 0.1 N HCl is

    A. 1	B. 10	C. 20	D. 25	E. 30

29. Calcification of the muscles is MOST likely due to

    A. hyperparathyroidism
    B. hypervitaminosis D
    C. neurotrophic atrophy
    D. vitamin E deficiency
    E. copper toxicity

30. ALL of the following substances cause a *decrease* in the stomach emptying rate EXCEPT

    A. excess acid
    B. fat and fatty acid
    C. hyperactivity of the duodenum
    D. secretin
    E. gastrin

KEY (CORRECT ANSWERS)

1.	D	16.	D
2.	D	17.	A
3.	D	18.	B
4.	A	19.	A
5.	A	20.	D
6.	C	21.	D
7.	B	22.	A
8.	D	23.	E
9.	E	24.	B
10.	B	25.	B
11.	A	26.	C
12.	D	27.	E
13.	A	28.	B
14.	A	29.	A
15.	B	30.	C

TEST 3

DIRECTIONS: Each question or incomplete statement is followed by several suggested answers or completions. Select the one that BEST answers the question or completes the statement. *PRINT THE LETTER OF THE CORRECT ANSWER IN THE SPACE AT THE RIGHT.*

1. The urine is *normally* alkaline in

   A. grass fed cows
   B. meat fed cat
   C. grain fed chicken
   D. starving cow
   E. meat fed dog

2. The hormone that enhances CHO metabolism by stimulating gluconeogenesis is

   A. aldosterone
   B. deoxycortisone
   C. cortisol
   D. insulin
   E. thyroxine

3. Oxygen is administered to a dog anesthetized with morphine sulfate and pentobarbital. The dog got apnea because

   A. *increased* O_2 in the blood inhibited his respiratory center
   B. O_2 potentiates respiratory depression
   C. O_2 removed the chemoreceptors drive for inspiration
   D. *increased* O_2 caused a *decrease* in CO_2 necessary to stimulate the respiratory center
   E. no relationship

4. An *increase* in cardiac output can be achieved by

   A. *increased* heart rate and *decreased* stroke volume
   B. *decreased* heart rate and *decreased* stroke volume
   C. *increased* heart rate and *increased* end diastolic volume
   D. *decreased* heart rate and *decreased* end diastolic volume
   E. *increased* heart rate and *increased* end systolic volume

5. Which of the following statements concerning terminal bronchi is *correct*?

   A. Diameter *increases* as lung volume *decreases*
   B. Diameter *increases* during forced expiration
   C. Cartilagenous rings are present
   D. Constrict in response to many stimuli
   E. Line by squamous epithelium

6. The *predominant* hormone in the bitch with pseudopregnancy is

   A. prolactin
   B. estrogen
   C. LH
   D. progesterone
   E. FSH

7. Which of the following is absorbed *fastest* in the small intestine of the dog?

   A. Ribose
   B. Xylose
   C. Galactose
   D. Sucrose
   E. Glucose

8. Of the following compounds, the MOST important source of gluconeogenesis is (are)   8.____

   A. acetyl CoA
   B. choline
   C. amino acids
   D. long chain fatty acids
   E. short chain fatty acids

9. Carbonic anhydrase is present within the erythrocyte and aids in the transport of carbon dioxide because it   9.____

   A. is an excellent buffer
   B. catalyzes the formation of carbonic acid
   C. catalyzes the deoxygenation of hemoglobin
   D. enables chloride ions to be transported into the erythrocyte
   E. catalyzes the formation of carbamino-hemoglobin

10. During normal quiet breathing, the expiratory movement of air is due *primarily* to   10.____

    A. contraction of elastin fibers in the alveoli
    B. contraction of abdominal muscles
    C. contraction of smooth muscle in the lungs
    D. passive relaxation of inspiratory muscles and elastic recoil of the lung
    E. relaxation and opening up of the larynx

11. A circulating catecholamine which is vasoconstrictive to the skin vasculature but vasodilative to skeletal muscles is   11.____

    A. serotonin
    B. acetylcholine
    C. angiotensin II
    D. epinephrine
    E. norepinephrine

12. The factors of *greatest* importance in the production of arterial blood pressure are   12.____

    A. arterial elasticity and size of the venous reservoir
    B. capillary pressure and venous return
    C. cardiac output and peripheral resistance
    D. capillary resistance and venous pressure
    E. blood viscosity and packed cell volume

13. The motor center of the sheep and goat brain is located in the   13.____

    A. velum of the medulla
    B. midbrain near the red nucleus
    C. thalamic area
    D. posterior hypothalamus
    E. frontal convulsion area near the cerebrum

14. Pseudounipolar neurons are found in the   14.____

    A. cochlear ganglion
    B. spinal ganglion
    C. corpus callosum
    D. parasympathetic ganglion
    E. sympathetic ganglion

15. Acetylcholine does NOT mediate the impulses at the

   A. sympathetic postganglionic nerve endings
   B. parasympathetic postganglionic nerve endings
   C. automomic ganglia
   D. secretory fibers at the eccrine and apocrine glands
   E. motor nerve endings at skeletal muscle

15.____

16. The cellular tapetum lucidum of the dog is located in the

   A. choroid   B. ciliary body   C. retina
   D. vitreous body E. lamina fusca

16.____

17. The uvea or vascular tunic of the eye is made up of the choroid, the ciliary body, and the

   A. retina   B. lens   C. cornea   D. sclera   E. iris

17.____

18. The cells of the intestinal lamina epithelialis mucosae have a replacement rate on the order of

   A. less than a week
   B. two to three weeks
   C. four to six weeks
   D. two to three months
   E. more than five months

18.____

19. Bilirubin, an excretory substance found in the bile, is a

   A. major end product of hemoglobin metabolism
   B. product of disintegration of the blood platelets
   C. derivative of endogenous cholesterol
   D. metabolite of plasma phospholipids
   E. precursor of the protein globin

19.____

20. The buffer system of the blood consists of

   A. several acid salts
   B. acid and alkaline salts
   C. weak acids and their alkaline salts
   D. a weak base and a weak acid
   E. a weak base and its acid salt

20.____

21. A characteristic of the composition of the glomerular filtrate which differentiates it from the composition of the blood plasma is the

   A. high concentration of anions
   B. low concentration of cations
   C. absence of erythrocytes
   D. virtual absence of protein
   E. high concentration of non-ionized crystalloids

21.____

22. The transfer of antibodies to offspring in the sow occurs   22._____

    A. *before* birth
    B. *after* birth
    C. only if there is a break in continuity of the mammary gland
    D. *neither* before nor after birth
    E. *both* before and after birth

23. The A-V oxygen difference between the renal artery and vein is LESS than that of the   23._____
    rest of the body.
    Using this isolated information, it can be said that

    A. the tubular epithelium is an inefficient O_2 utilizer
    B. the tubular epithelium absorbs much O_2 from the glomerular filtrate
    C. the kidney has a *low* O_2 requirement
    D. the kidney receives ample O_2 supply
    E. the metabolic rate of the kidney parenchyma is *high*

24. The HCl in the stomach has a pH of approximately 1. This is equivalent to a concentra-   24._____
    tion of 0.1 N. HCl has a specific gravity of 1.19 for an assay of 37%.
    How much concentrated HC_2 is needed to make 1 liter of 0.1 NH_4Cl?

    A. 1 ml.   B. 10 ml.   C. 100 ml.   D. 1 liter   E. 10 liter

25. Centrosomes play a part in   25._____

    A. DNA synthesis   B. RNA synthesis
    C. protein synthesis   D. secretory activity
    E. cellular division

26. The development of urethral calculi in steers seems to be due to   26._____

    A. vitamin A deficiency
    B. insufficient water intake
    C. pre-existing urinary infection
    D. mineral imbalances
    E. multifactorial causes

27. Gas evacuated by the ruminant is   27._____

    A. lost *entirely* through the nose and mouth
    B. *partially* passed in to the lungs and trachea
    C. a *common* cause of frothy blood
    D. a major metabolic loss
    E. all nitrogen

28. Fats absorbed from the small intestine into the lacteals are *mostly* in the form of   28._____

    A. glycerol and fatty acids
    B. low density lipoproteins
    C. chylomicrons
    D. monoglycerides and fatty acids
    E. monoglycerides, diglycerides and fatty acids

29. What effect will dicoumarol have on whole blood which has been withdrawn from the vasculature?

   A. Slow coagulation
   B. Prevent coagulation
   C. Cause lysis instead of coagulation
   D. Speed coagulation
   E. No effect

30. Fertilization in domestic animals *usually* occurs in the

   A. vagina
   B. cervix
   C. body of uterus
   D. horns of uterus
   E. oviduct

KEY (CORRECT ANSWERS)

1. A	16. A
2. D	17. E
3. C	18. A
4. C	19. A
5. D	20. C
6. D	21. D
7. E	22. B
8. A	23. B
9. B	24. B
10. D	25. E
11. D	26. E
12. C	27. B
13. B	28. C
14. B	29. E
15. B	30. E

EXAMINATION SECTION
TEST 1

DIRECTIONS: Each question consists of a statement. You are to indicate whether the statement is TRUE (T) or FALSE (F). *PRINT THE LETTER OF THE CORRECT ANSWER IN THE SPACE AT THE RIGHT.*

1. ALL pneumococci fall into one or 32 types. 1.____

2. 0.5 cc of serum plus 9.5 cc of saline makes a 1:20 dilution. 2.____

3. ALL pathogenic intestinal bacteria are lactose fermenters. 3.____

4. To test the virulence of C. diphtheriae found in cultures of nose and throat, a pure culture must ALWAYS be obtained. 4.____

5. Pneumococci are the ONLY organism sufficiently important to identify in the sputum from pneumonia patients. 5.____

6. The presence of acid-fast bacilli in voided urine is proof of infection with tubercle bacilli. 6.____

7. Some of the Staph. can produce food poisoning. 7.____

8. Escherichi coli is ALWAYS a contaminant when found in blood cultures. 8.____

9. Bacillary dysentery is caused only by Shigella dysenteriae. 9.____

10. Fluid thioglycollate medium is considered the medium of choice for sterility tests as it supports the growth of both aerobic and anaerobic bacteria. 10.____

11. The differentiation between the Coli aerogenes group of organisms and those of the Salmonella-Shigella group is based on fermentation reactions. 11.____

12. Members of the genus Salmonella may produce human infection and may be isolated from the bloodstream early in the disease. 12.____

13. When looking for a dysentery organism, it is good practice to incubate feces in an enrichment broth for a few hours. 13.____

14. Borrelia recurrentis may be demonstrated in the blood of a person with relapsing fever. 14.____

15. Gentian violet is a suitable stain for demonstrating relapsing fever spirochaetes in the blood smear. 15.____

16. Gram's iodine solution does NOT deteriorate on standing. 16.____

2 (#1)

17. The fermentation of lactose is one characteristic that distinguishes members of the Salmonella group from S. typhosa. 17.____

18. Lactose and mannitol are sugars which serve to separate the genus Shigella into three groups. 18.____

19. Thick blood smears are difficult to examine and should NOT be used in preference to thin smears in the diagnosis of relapsing fever. 19.____

20. The gram stain is an important reaction in the identification of the cocci. 20.____

21. The addition of 1% dextrose to blood agar plates prevents the Beta hemolytic strep from forming hemolytic colonies. 21.____

22. Strep isolated from cases of scarlet fever and septic sore throat can be readily distinguished by their cultural characteristics. 22.____

23. Lancefield grouping and typing is the MOST useful means of differentiating beta hemolytic strep from human sources. 23.____

24. Brownian movement is NOT observed if the bacteria in the suspension are dead. 24.____

25. The demonstration that many viruses produce plaques is of basic importance because it provides a means of measuring virus size. 25.____

KEY (CORRECT ANSWERS)

1.	F		11.	T
2.	T		12.	T
3.	F		13.	F
4.	T		14.	T
5.	F		15.	F
6.	F		16.	F
7.	T		17.	F
8.	F		18.	F
9.	F		19.	T
10.	T		20.	T

21.	T
22.	F
23.	T
24.	F
25.	F

TEST 2

DIRECTIONS: Each question or incomplete statement is followed by several suggested answers or completions. Select the one that BEST answers the question or completes the statement. *PRINT THE LETTER OF THE CORRECT ANSWER IN THE SPACE AT THE RIGHT.*

1. Bacteriophages are intermediate in size between a virus and rickettsiae.   1.____

2. M. tuberculosis will grow ONLY under aerobic conditions.   2.____

3. ALL motile bacteria possess flagella.   3.____

4. The bacterial spore is PRIMARILY a means of reproduction.   4.____

5. MOST pathogenic bacteria are basophilic.   5.____

6. Dry heat at 180° for 30 minutes is satisfactory sterilizing glassware.   6.____

7. Albert's stain is suitable for staining C. diphtheriae.   7.____

8. Bacillus anthracis are gram positive.   8.____

9. An identification of B. anthracis is BEST made on the basis of fermentation reactions.   9.____

10. Brucella abortus is transmitted in raw milk.   10.____

11. Pasteurization of milk will destroy Brucella organisms.   11.____

12. H. abortus is BEST isolated on tryptose agar medium.   12.____

13. The opsonocytophagic index is used in the diagnosis of brucellosis.   13.____

14. C. perfringens (Welchii) is BEST grown under anaerobic conditions.   14.____

15. C. perfringens when grown on blood agar does NOT produce hemolysis.   15.____

16. The spores of C. tetani are killed by freezing at 32°.   16.____

17. C. tetani usually produces central spores.   17.____

18. Hemolytic coliform bacteria may be found in the urine.   18.____

19. The presence of Lactose-fermenting organisms in a water supply indicates fecal contamination.   19.____

20. Typhoid organisms produce H_2S on Klinger's Iron Agar media.   20.____

2 (#2)

21. The typhoid organisms can be isolated from the bloodstream during typhoid fever.   21.____

22. Sucrose may be added to Klinger's Iron Agar for MORE rapid identification of the paracolon group of bacteria.   22.____

23. E. coli produces a negative citrate utilization test.   23.____

24. Salmonella paratyphi usually produces NO gas in the butt of Russell's double agar.   24.____

25. For the isolation of Shigella dysenteriae, it is essential to have the culture media exactly isotonic   25.____

KEY (CORRECT ANSWERS)

1.	F		11.	T
2.	F		12.	F
3.	F		13.	F
4.	F		14.	T
5.	F		15.	T
6.	T		16.	F
7.	T		17.	F
8.	T		18.	T
9.	F		19.	T
10.	T		20.	T

21.	T
22.	F
23.	T
24.	F
25.	F

TEST 3

DIRECTIONS: Each question or incomplete statement is followed by several suggested answers or completions. Select the one that BEST answers the question or completes the statement. *PRINT THE LETTER OF THE CORRECT ANSWER IN THE SPACE AT THE RIGHT.*

1. Species of brucella are probably BEST differentiated by bacteriostatic effect of dyes.   1.____

2. Salmonella pullorum contain only *H* antigens and NO *O* antigens because the organism is flagellar.   2.____

3. Animal pathogenicity tests are *most commonly* used for the differentiation of the species of tuberculosis organisms.   3.____

4. The *test-tube brush* effect in a gelatin tube is rarely used for the identification of Erysipelothrix rhusiopathiae.   4.____

5. An invitro method usually used for differentiating pathogenic from non-pathogenic staphylococci is the coagulase test.   5.____

6. Pathogenic staphylococci are categorized using phage typing.   6.____

7. Salmonella ferment lactose and dextrose.   7.____

8. Salmonella produces indole from certain amino acids.   8.____

9. Johne's disease is transmissible to humans.   9.____

10. Hemophilia in dogs is due to the absence of plasma factor for making thromboplastin available.   10.____

11. Toxins of Cl. botulinum can be differentiated by specific neutralization with mouse inoculation.   11.____

12. Foot and mouth disease is NOT contagious.   12.____

13. Oxygen is necessary for the growth of the tetanus bacilli.   13.____

14. Salmonella cholerasuis causes infectious swine enteritis in hogs.   14.____

15. Johne's disease is characterized by hemorrhage, thickening and wrinkling of the cecum, colon, and rectum.   15.____

16. In studying viruses, the purpose of alternate passage is to adapt the virus to an experimental host.   16.____

17. In the treatment of bluetongue, ONLY infected animals need be vaccinated.   17.____

18. Borrelia anserine causes disease in geese ONLY. 18.____

19. Swine are susceptible to ALL forms of TB. 19.____

20. Laboratory utensils should NOT be sterilized with flame or autoclave. 20.____

21. Listeria monocytogenes appear on blood agar as circular, smooth, transparent, and gray. 21.____

22. In washing a Gram stain with old distilled water, the gram positive organisms will be decolorized due to bacterial contamination in the water. 22.____

23. Staph. can ALWAYS be differentiated from strep. by microscopic exam. 23.____

24. Undulant fever, Malta fever, and Mediterranean fever are synonyms for brucellosis. 24.____

25. The ring test is used to determine the presence of agglutination antibodies for Brucella abortus in milk. It is used on pooler herd samples and serves as an excellent screening test for the location of Brucella-carrying cows. 25.____

KEY (CORRECT ANSWERS)

1.	T	11.	T
2.	F	12.	F
3.	T	13.	F
4.	F	14.	T
5.	T	15.	T
6.	T	16.	T
7.	F	17.	F
8.	F	18.	F
9.	F	19.	T
10.	T	20.	F

21.	T
22.	F
23.	F
24.	F
25.	T

EXAMINATION SECTION
TEST 1

DIRECTIONS: Each question consists of a statement. You are to indicate whether the statement is TRUE (T) or FALSE (F). *PRINT THE LETTER OF THE CORRECT ANSWER IN THE SPACE AT THE RIGHT.*

1. Microsporum and trichophyton can be differentiated since microsporum usually fluoresces and trichophyton does NOT. 1.____

2. Episiotomy is enlarging the external genital opening. 2.____

3. Systemic lupus is a multisystemic disease frequently resulting in terminal renal failure. 3.____

4. The Voges-Proskauer reaction is a test for acetyl-methyl-carbinol. 4.____

5. Penicillinase is a form of penicillin. 5.____

6. The plating of a fecal specimen immediately *after* collection increases the chances of recovery of enteric pathogens. 6.____

7. The Koch-Weeks bacillus is the cause of Trachoma. 7.____

8. The cultivation of N. gonorrhea is BEST carried out in an atmosphere devoid of oxygen. 8.____

9. Darkfield examination of serum from a suspected skin lesion is the MOST dependable means of identifying asyphilitic chancre. 9.____

10. Nocardia has culture characteristics of anaerobic acid fast. 10.____

11. Actinomyces bovis is BEST cultivated on plain agar plates. 11.____

12. Anthrax is a disease that can be contracted from wool. 12.____

13. Proteus OX 19 is the causative organism of Rocky Mountain Spotted Fever. 13.____

14. Borrelia vincentii is gram positive. 14.____

15. The vaccine used to immunize for equine encephalomyelitis consists of purified whole embryo killed vaccine. 15.____

16. Dordelein's bacilli are part of the normal vaginal flora, 16.____

17. ALL diphtheriae bearing polar granules stained with Albert's stain are C. diphtheriae. 17.____

18. The finding of a gram negative intracellular diploeocci in a smear of pus from a cervical smear is *always* N. gonorrhea. 18.____

19. C. diphtheriae when stained by Gram's method will decolorize easily but the granules will remain gram positive. 19.____

20. The bacillus of TB is readily killed by 5% NaOH. 20.____

21. In the Lancefield system of classification, most of the human pathogens are classified in group *A*. 21.____

22. Anthrax blood shows gram + rods with NO spores. 22.____

23. The MOST common characteristic of myxo-viruses is their ability to agglutinate red blood cells. 23.____

24. Histomonas melengridis is the parasite involved in entero-hepatitis in turkeys. 24.____

25. The cause of red mange in the dog is demodex folliculorum. 25.____

KEY (CORRECT ANSWERS)

1.	T	11.	F
2.	T	12.	T
3.	T	13.	F
4.	T	14.	F
5.	F	15.	T
6.	T	16.	T
7.	F	17.	F
8.	F	18.	F
9.	T	19.	T
10.	F	20.	F

21.	T
22.	T
23.	T
24.	T
25.	T

TEST 2

DIRECTIONS: Each question consists of a statement. You are to indicate whether the statement is TRUE (T) or FALSE (F). *PRINT THE LETTER OF THE CORRECT ANSWER IN THE SPACE AT THE RIGHT.*

1. Moraxella bovis causes inflammation of the cornea and conjunctiva. 1.____

2. Microsporum canis infection in cats is often NOT diagnosed because carrier animals do NOT manifest clinical signs. 2.____

3. Hog cholera and African swine fever are diseases that are related serologically. 3.____

4. Dermatomycosis of the bovine is caused by mites. 4.____

5. Fowl typhoid is caused by S. gallinarium. 5.____

6. Growth of brucella abortus is enhanced by certain concentration of CO_2. 6.____

7. Desoxycholate agar is a suitable media for the isolation of S. typhi. 7.____

8. *Sulfur granules* are colonies of actinomyces bovis. 8.____

9. Thrush is an infection with condida albicans. 9.____

10. Salmonella cholerasuis is believed to cause infectious enteritis in swine. 10.____

11. Thioglychollate medium produces both aerobic and relatively anaerobic conditions. 11.____

12. The oxidase reaction is useful for separating N. gonorrhea from N. intracellularis. 12.____

13. N. catarrhalis is *always* present in nasal secretions. 13.____

14. Leptospira icterohemorrhagiea is regarded as being the cause of Weil's disease. 14.____

15. Cough plates for the isolation of whooping cough organisms contains approximately 20% blood. 15.____

16. Meat extract agars enhance salmonella growth. 16.____

17. Tuberculosis bacilli are differentiated by injection of organisms into guinea pigs *only*. 17.____

18. Black leg in cattle is caused by Clostridium chauvais. Animals showing symptoms of black leg should be segregated to prevent the spread of the disease. 18.____

19. Enterotosemia may be diagnosed by testing for clostridial antibodies by ppt test. 19.____

20. An important point to remember with ascarid prevention in general is that ascarid eggs are very resistant to environmental conditions and may withstand extremely cold temperatures, 20.____

21. In the dog, the flea is the internal host for diplydium caninum. 21.____

22. The agglutination lysis test is used in lepto. 22.____

23. Actinobacillus does NOT invade soft tissue. 23.____

24. Potato agar and liver infusion are used to isolate brucella. 24.____

25. A pregnant owner of a cat should be advised that toxo-plasmosis CANNOT be transmitted to humans and .trans-placental fetal transmission is impossible. 25.____

KEY (CORRECT ANSWERS)

1. T   11. F
2. T   12. F
3. F   13. F
4. F   14. T
5. T   15. T

6. T   16. T
7. T   17. F
8. T   18. T
9. T   19. T
10. T   20. T

21. T
22. T
23. F
24. T
25. F

EXAMINATION SECTION
TEST 1

Questions 1-16.

DIRECTIONS: Answer the following questions directly, briefly, and succinctly.

1. What is the physical state of the media on which leptospira can be cultured? 1._____
2. What is the MOST common cause of paratyphoid in turkeys? 2._____
3. What substance is required by PPLO as a medium for growth? 3._____
4. What atmosphere does brucella abortis require for BEST growth? 4._____
5. What are the BEST disinfectants for bacteria? 5._____
6. How many viruses cause Equine Encephalomyelitis? 6._____
7. What organism is *most commonly* isolated by blood culture from cows? 7._____
8. What organism is BEST diagnosed from fresh, unfixed, unstained smear of tissue? 8._____
9. Where does Leptospira localize? 9._____
10. What type of irradiation is BEST for sterilization? 10._____
11. What causes Q fever? 11._____
12. What kind of toxin is produced by C. tetani? 12._____
13. How is actinomycosis diagnosed bacteriologically? 13._____
14. What is the MOST common cause of ringworm in cats? 14._____
15. What is the lesion in the brain of cattle with listeriosis? 15._____
16. What important physiological characteristic of Bacillus antracie is important to remember in preventing contamination and spread of the organism? 16._____

Questions 17-35.

DIRECTIONS: Fill in the blank space(s) the word (or words) which is (are) the correct answer(s) to the question.

17. The cause of aspergillosis in chickens is aspergillus _____. 17._____
18. The organism MOST resistant to heat and causing a problem in pasteurization is _____. 18._____
19. The BEST stain for anaplasma is _____. 19._____
20. The BEST medium for the isolation of salmonella is _____. 20._____
21. The direct effect of fresh homologous antiserum on living spirochetes is _____. 21._____

22. The causative agent for fowl typhoid is _____. 22.____

23. The MOST frequently reported bacterial disease is _____. 23.____

24. A group of chicks, 4-5 weeks old, are presented. Some are dead, and some are paralyzed, with fine muscle tremors. The *probable* diagnosis is _____. 24.____

25. In viruses with nucleic acid, RNA is for antigenic activity and _____. 25.____

26. The cytoplasm inoclusions known as Bollinger Bodies may be found in stained histopathological section prepared from animal infection of _____. 26.____

27. Anthrax in the United States is *commonly* transmitted by _____. 27.____

28. Nucleic acids of RNA viruses are responsible for _____. 28.____

29. Weil's disease is caused by _____. 29.____

30. Viruses are identified in tissue culture by _____. 30.____

31. The camp test is used to diagnose _____. 31.____

32. The species whose serum has the MOST complement is the _____. 32.____

33. The MINIMUM temperature required to kill spiroehetes in 10 minutes is at least _____. 33.____

34. The cause of Gid in sheep is _____. 34.____

35. Lepto is differentiated by _____. 35.____

KEY (CORRECT ANSWERS)

1. Liquid
2. Salmonella typhimurium
3. Serum
4. CO_2 atmosphere
5. Halogens
6. Two
7. C. pyogenes
8. Leptospirosis
9. The urinary tract
10. Ultraviolet
11. Coxiella burnetti
12. Exotoxin
13. Anaerobic culture
14. Microsporum canis
15. Microabscess in the brain
16. O_2 is necessary for sporulation
17. fumigatus
18. rickettsia burnetti
19. Gram's stain
20. selenite plate
21. clumps
22. salmonella gallinarium
23. salmonella
24. avian encephalomyelitis
25. replication
26. fowl pox
27. soil
28. carrying the genetic code of the virus
29. leptospira icterohemorrhagica
30. cytopathic effects on tissue culture cells
31. strep. ag.
32. guinea pig
33. 50 - 60°C
34. multiceps
35. serology

TEST 2

Questions 1-14.

DIRECTIONS: Answer the following questions directly, briefly, and succinctly.

1. What is the MOST important insect vector of equine encephoneyeliti?   1.____
2. Where are whipworms found?   2.____
3. What is the MOST common sheep parasite?   3.____
4. Where is the choroid plexus found in the dog?   4.____
5. What is the MAIN artery to the rumen?   5.____
6. How many pairs of legs does the adult insect have?   6.____
7. What disease do ducks showing G.I. lesions, *annular rings,* focal areas of necrosis, and enteritis have?   7.____
8. What is the treatment for adult heartworm?   8.____
9. What agent aids in transmission of swine influenza virus?   9.____
10. During what season is treatment of a horse with bots BEST performed?   10.____
11. After worming an animal for intestinal parasites (hookworm), how long should you wait before checking the stool for ova?   11.____
12. What animal is MOST infected with psoroptie ear mite?   12.____
13. What causes dermatomycosis of the bovine?   13.____
14. What is the cause of avian spirochetosis in the U.S.?   14.____

Questions 15-35

DIRECTIONS: Fill in the blank space(s) the word (or words) which is (are) the correct answer(s) to the question.

15. Chiggers are _____.   15.____
16. The cause of dourine is the sporozoan parasite _____.   16.____
17. Adult hookworms are found in the _____.   17.____
18. Babesia piroplasma bigemina causes _____.   18.____
19. The three types of cattle mange are the _____.   19.____
20. Transfer due to an active effort on the part of the parasite, with emphasis on the invasion of the new host is _____.   20.____
21. Trypanosome disease in the U.S. is tested by _____.   21.____
22. A drug that is effective for whipworms in the dog is _____.   22.____

23. In the horse, S. vulgaris in the cranial mesenteric artery causes _____.   23.____

24. Neorickettsia relminthoeca causes _____.   24.____

25. Double operculate ova in intestinal seapings of chickens are due to _____.   25.____

26. The infectious disease of cattle caused by anaplasma marginale and characterized by progressive anemia due to destruction of erythrocytes is _____.   26.____

27. The term *hard tick for* I oxidol refers to the _____.   27.____

28. Dermatophytic fungi cause _____.   28.____

29. Spirocerca lupi causes _____.   29.____

30. Summer sores is BEST described as _____.   30.____

31. The *only* mite that is transmissible to other animals or man is _____.   31.____

32. The rickettsia MOST resistant to drying is _____.   32.____

33. The nematode responsible for MOST cases of cutaneous larval is _____.   33.____

34. The larva of toxacara canis in humans is called _____.   34.____

35. The _____ horsefly can suck blood.   35.____

KEY (CORRECT ANSWERS)

1. Mosquitoes
2. In the cecum and colon
3. Haemonchus contortus
4. 4th ventricle brain
5. Celiac artery
6. 3
7. Duck viral enteritis
8. Thiacetarsamide
9. Earthworm
10. Mid-winter
11. 10 days
12. Rabbit
13. Fungus
14. Borrelia anserina
15. larval mites
16. trypanosona equiperdum
17. small intestine
18. Texas fever
19. saroptic, psoroptic and chorioptic types
20. active transfer
21. complement fixation test
22. whipcide (phthalofyne) at a dose of 250 mg/kg orally or I.V.
23. verminous colic
24. salmon disease
25. capillaria
26. anaplasmosis
27. scutum
28. ringworm
29. fibrosarcoma
30. cutaneous habronemiasis
31. sarcoptes
32. coxiella burnetti
33. ancylostoma braziliense
34. visceral larval migrans
35. female

EXAMINATION SECTION
TEST 1

DIRECTIONS: Each question or incomplete statement is followed by several suggested answers or completions. Select the one that BEST answers the question or completes the statement. *PRINT THE LETTER OF THE CORRECT ANSWER IN THE SPACE AT THE RIGHT.*

1. A nematode parasite which in its adult stage inhabits the bronchioles of cattle is

    A. dictyocaulus filaria
    B. metastrongylus apri
    C. dictyocaulus arnfieldi
    D. dictyocaulus viviparus
    E. haemonchus contortus

2. The *same* animal may serve as *both* definitive and intermediate host for

    A. fasciola hepatica
    B. taenia pisiformis
    C. dipylidium caninum
    D. trichinella spiralis
    E. anoplocephala magna

3. Which of the following animals may play a role in the transmission of toxoplasmosis to humans?

    A. dog
    B. canary
    C. parrot
    D. parakeet
    E. cat

4. ALL of the following parasites have been shown to infect nursing young via the colostrum or milk of the mother EXCEPT

    A. trichuris vulpis of dogs
    B. toxocara cati of cats
    C. strongyloides ransomi of pigs
    D. ancylostoma caninum of dogs
    E. toxocara canis of dogs

5. The MOST common helminth infection encountered in mice is that produced by

    A. taenia taeniaformis
    B. enterobius SP
    C. syphacia SP or aspiculuris SP
    D. hymenolepis nana or lanceolata
    E. trichuris SP

6. Diagnosis of fascioloides magna in cattle is *usually* accomplished by

    A. a blood test
    B. post mortem examination
    C. fecal flotation
    D. a complement fixation test
    E. fecal sedimentation

7. The *preferred* medium for oviposition of cochliomyia americanum (callitroga hominovorax) is

    A. stacked or piled horse manure
    B. fresh cow manure
    C. decaying vegetation
    D. a dead and decomposing carcass
    E. a fresh wound, cut, or laceration

8. An adult fly that does NOT bite or feed on the host animal it attacks is

   A. gastrophilus nasalis
   B. simulium venustum
   C. stomoxys calcitrans
   D. tabanus atratus
   E. siphona (haematobia) irritans

9. Mites were recovered from the area of the root of the tail and udder attachment (escutcheon) of three dairy cattle in one herd. Pruritis and dermatitis were mild. What is the MOST probable etiology?

   A. Demodex bovis
   B. Sarcoptes scabiei
   C. Psoroptes communis var. bovis
   D. Psorergates bovis
   E. Chorioptes bovis

10. The mosquito is the intermediate host of

    A. dirofilaria immitis
    B. dipetalonema reconditum
    C. onchocerca volvulus
    D. leishmania braziliensis
    E. leucocytozoon smithi

11. Auricular acariasis is NOT uncommonly diagnosed in the five species of animal hosts listed below. In FOUR of these host animals, the parasite is otodectes cynotis. Which one suffers from psoroptic ear infestation?

    A. Fox   B. Dog   C. Cat   D. Rabbit   E. Ferret

12. An infected individual that harbors a specific infectious agent in the absence of discernible clinical disease and serves as a potential source of infection for susceptibles is a

    A. vehicle   B. reservoir   C. case
    D. vector   E. carrier

13. The MOST frequent mode of spread of anthrax among domestic animals is

    A. ingestion of sporulated organisms
    B. inhalation of airborne spores
    C. cutaneous contact with convalescent animals
    D. deep emplacement of vegetative organisms in wounds
    E. the bite of blood-sucking insects or ticks

14. The incubation period in scrapie, a nonfebrile, fatal, chronic disease of sheep, is

    A. less than 7 days   B. 7-14 days
    C. 1-2 months   D. 3-6 months
    E. over 6 months

15. Hydatidosis is caused by infestation with 15.____

   A. multiceps multiceps
   B. taenia saginata
   C. echinococcus granulosus
   D. dipylidium caninum
   E. taenia solium

16. One of the MOST reliable procedures for surveying exposure to toxoplasmosis in man 16.____
    and animals in various regions of the United States is the

   A. fluorescent antibody technique
   B. Sabin-Feldman dye test
   C. capillary tube agglutination test
   D. intradermal skin test
   E. MCAN precipitin test

17. The wildlife species in the midwestern United States in which rabies virus infection is 17.____
    MOST prevalent is the

   A. raccoon   B. fox   C. coyote
   D. skunk   E. bat

18. Leptospirosis is a bacterial disease of domestic animals that is transmissible from the 18.____
    infected host to humans. It is *generally* accepted that the bacteria from the infected animal are transmitted to the susceptible host by

   A. consumption of unpasteurized milk from infected udders
   B. contact with feces, especially during periods of diarrhea
   C. contact with airborne moisture droplets from nasal discharges
   D. contact with the urine from infected kidneys
   E. consumption of meat and other edible tissues

19. A diagnosis of foot-and-mouth disease on a farm would require quarantine of 19.____

   A. the infected animals *only*
   B. ALL animals, animal products, hay, and grain on that farm and ALL adjoining farms
   C. ALL animals until they have been appraised and slaughtered
   D. ALL animals and animal products on the farm known to be infected, as well as on ALL adjoining farms
   E. ALL animals, but permitting milk to be sold where dairy cattle are involved

20. In the United States, the disease of cattle which is characterized by symptoms similar to 20.____
    those of rinderpest is

   A. bovine viral diarrhea-mucosal disease
   B. vesicular stomatitis
   C. parainfluenza-3 infection
   D. infectious bovine rhinotracheitis
   E. malignant catarrhal fever

21. The control of caseous lymphadenitis in sheep is *generally* based on the use of

   A. pesticides to reduce ectoparasite numbers
   B. hygiene during shearing and docking
   C. an autogenous staphylococcus aureus bacterin
   D. a corynebacterium pyogenes bacterin
   E. pasture rotation and age segregation

22. The protein coat or shell of the viral particle is called the

   A. unit membrane
   B. limiting membrane
   C. cell wall
   D. envelope
   E. capsid

23. The biggest fault with veterinary antihelmintic is that it

   A. does NOT affect the larval stage
   B. *increases* susceptibility to reinfection
   C. is toxic and prescription needed
   D. irritates already inflamed mucosa
   E. suppresses inflammatory response

24. The MOST likely carnivore to infect man with trichinella spiralis is the

   A. black bear
   B. domestic cat
   C. dog
   D. spotted skunk
   E. red-tail fox

25. The term ECOLOGY defines the study of

   A. populations and their interactions with their environment
   B. host species and their roles in social structures
   C. pollution and its control
   D. symbiosis between dissimilar organisms
   E. climactic factors like temperature and rainfall and their influence on seasons

KEY (CORRECT ANSWERS)

1. D	11. D	21. B
2. D	12. E	22. E
3. E	13. A	23. A
4. A	14. E	24. A
5. D	15. C	25. A
6. B	16. B	
7. E	17. D	
8. A	18. D	
9. E	19. B	
10. A	20. A	

TEST 2

DIRECTIONS: Each question or incomplete statement is followed by several suggested answers or completions. Select the one that BEST answers the question or completes the statement. *PRINT THE LETTER OF THE CORRECT ANSWER IN THE SPACE AT THE RIGHT.*

1. The *Mallein Test* and the *Straus Reaction* are useful for the recognition of

    A. cholera   B. anthrax   C. leprosy
    D. glanders   E. dengue

2. Borrelia anserina causes disease in

    A. rabbits   B. dogs   C. chickens
    D. horses   E. cows

3. An antibiotic that may be added to inhibit saprophytic fungal contaminants in a media intended for cultivation of fungal pathogens is

    A. penicillin   B. streptomycin   C. tetracycline
    D. panmycin   E. acti-dione

4. The MOST common bacterial organism found in genital infections in horses is

    A. escherichia coli
    B. streptococcus zooepidemicus
    C. salmonella abortus equi
    D. actinobacillus (shigella) equuli
    E. streptococcus equi

5. What should be done with a hog slaughtered that has diamond skin lesions and no systemic involvement?

    A. Condemn it
    B. Make into animal food
    C. Pass and trim affected parts
    D. Pass for cooking
    E. Make into fertilizer

6. Rabies eradication is difficult in the U.S. because

    A. of the reservoir in native fauna
    B. of the reservoir in commensal rodents
    C. some strains don't produce Negri bodies
    D. the vaccine is not efficacious
    E. of the long latent period in domestic animals

7. Hemoglobinuria occurs in ALL of the following diseases of animals EXCEPT

    A. piroplasmosis
    B. bracken fern
    C. anaplasmosis
    D. post parturient hemoglobinuria
    E. bacillary hemoglobinuria

8. After 90 days in a breeding herd (beef) of 250 head with 15 bulls, 50% of the animals are still showing evidence of heat.
   The MOST probable cause is

   A. lepto
   B. nutritional
   C. vibrio
   D. hormone problem
   E. sperm abnormalities

9. Juvenile osteodystrophy (nutritional osteodystrophy, osteogenesis imperfecta):

   A. Affects *both* dogs and cats
   B. Results *primarily* from a deficiency of calcium caused by a dietary imbalance
   C. Is characterized radiographically by a generalized skeletal osteoporosis with extremely thin bone cortices
   D. All of the above
   E. None of the above

10. The cranial nerve necessary for the control of the diameter of the pupil is the _____ nerve.

    A. oculomotor
    B. abducent
    C. hypoglossal
    D. trigeminal
    E. vagus

11. The paired bodies of erectile tissue of the penis are called corpora

    A. arenacaea
    B. albicans
    C. cavernosa penis
    D. lutea
    E. cavernosa urethrae

12. Urinary infections are MORE common in female animals because of

    A. their more constricted urethra
    B. their more dilated urethra
    C. the effect of estrogen on the bladder
    D. the effect of FSH on the bladder wall
    E. the effect of LH on the bladder

13. Specific infectious pyelonephritis of the cow is caused by

    A. actinomycosis bovis
    B. clostridium septicum
    C. staphylococcus aureus
    D. cornyebacterium pyogenes
    E. corynebacterium renale

14. A bovine hemolytic disease transmitted by insects WITHOUT hemoglobinuria is

    A. anaplasmosis
    B. lepto
    C. piroplasmosis
    D. lympho
    E. hemolyticum septicum

15. Leucocytozoonosis of ducks and turkeys is transmitted by

    A. ticks
    B. lice
    C. flies
    D. mosquitos
    E. midges (simulidae)

16. Abortion due to T. fetus occurs during the

    A. first trimester
    B. second trimester
    C. last trimester
    D. last week
    E. first half

17. Virus pig pneumonia is maintained in herds *largely* through

    A. live virus vaccine
    B. ectoparasites
    C. lung worms
    D. birds and rodents
    E. carrier sows

18. Control of caseous lymphadenitis in sheep is *generally* based on the use of

    A. pesticides to reduce ectoparasites in number
    B. hygiene during shearing and docking
    C. autogenous staph aureus bacteria
    D. corynebacterium pyogenes bacterin
    E. pasture rotation and age separation

19. *Measly* beef is affected with

    A. cysticercus bovis
    B. cysticercus cellulosae
    C. coenuris
    D. pentastomum denticulatum
    E. trichinella spiralis

20. In the pasteurization of raw milk, the temperature is held continuously at 161°F for _____ seconds.

    A. 5   B. 10   C. 12   D. 15   E. 20

21. The MOST characteristic sign of allergic dermatitis is

    A. pruritis
    B. alopecia
    C. pain
    D. excessive exfoliation
    E. pustules

22. Suckling mice are used in the isolation of _____ viruses.

    A. arbo   B. adeno   C. pox   D. parvo   E. herpes

23. Negri bodies are pathognomonic for

    A. canine distemper
    B. cow pox
    C. rabies
    D. bluetongue
    E. rinderpest

24. The presence of an intestinal fluke is necessary for

    A. ovine conjunctivitis
    B. tickborne fever (dog)
    C. tickborne fever (sheep)
    D. salmon disease
    E. skin bone disease

25. Upon physical examination of a herd, mastitis is found. One that has fibrosis of the udder and bad milk   25.____

    A. passes unrestricted
    B. is treated with antibiotics
    C. is isolated and treated
    D. is condemned
    E. passes with restrictions

KEY (CORRECT ANSWERS)

1.	D	11.	C
2.	C	12.	B
3.	A	13.	E
4.	B	14.	A
5.	C	15.	E
6.	A	16.	B
7.	C	17.	E
8.	C	18.	B
9.	D	19.	A
10.	A	20.	D

21. A
22. E
23. C
24. D
25. D

EXAMINATION SECTION
TEST 1

DIRECTIONS: Each question or incomplete statement is followed by several suggested answers or completions. Select the one that BEST answers the question or completes the statement. *PRINT THE LETTER OF THE CORRECT ANSWER IN THE SPACE AT THE RIGHT.*

1. Veterinary inspections are maintained at approximately 60 major stockyards and several thousand auction markets throughout the country to   1.____

    A. determine health conditions and disease trends
    B. of livestock moving both interstate and intrastate
    C. test ALL animals for disease
    D. prevent diseased animals from entering markets
    E. prevent violations of state laws

2. Which of the following does NOT apply to a tuberculosis free accredited herd?   2.____

    A. MUST be tested every 6 months to maintain its status
    B. NO animal that has been designated a reactor at any time shall be retested
    C. The official tuberculin test shall be the intraderal test
    D. MUST pass a negative test within 14 months from the previous accreditation test to qualify for reaccreditation

3. Tuberculosis and brucellosis tests of cattle for export MUST be completed within _____ of the date of movement from the premises of origin.   3.____

    A. 30 days   B. 3 weeks   C. 3 months   D. 60 days

4. The cooperative state-federal brucellosis eradication program is designed to   4.____

    A. maintain constant surveillance and control of brucellosis in cattle only
    B. eradicate brucellosis from cattle only
    C. use continuous vaccination, surveillance, and control measures to keep a minimum incidence of brucellosis in livestock
    D. eradicate brucellosis from ALL livestock

5. An animal that has been designated a reactor to the tuberculin test   5.____

    A. MUST be tagged and branded and promptly removed from the herd
    B. should be kept until the calf is weaned
    C. may be isolated and retested by a regularly employed state or federal veterinarian
    D. may be retested in 60 days by the accredited veterinarian

6. Federal regulations concerning the hog cholera eradication program   6.____

    A. restrict intrastate movement of hogs
    B. establish inspection procedures and procedures for treating healthy, unexposed feeding and breeding swine moving interstate
    C. permit interstate shipment of slaughter hogs affected with hog cholera, if the hogs are consigned to a slaughter establishment operating under federal inspection
    D. permit interstate shipment of hogs fed raw garbage

7. In performing a tuberculin test

    A. history is MORE important than the reaction
    B. a needle NOT over 1/8 inch long should be used
    C. tuberculin should be injected intradermally
    D. tuberculin should be injected subcutaneously

8. Leptospirosis in cattle

    A. lends itself to an eradication program because the vaccine is very effective
    B. is a reportable disease and federal indemnity is available in local control programs
    C. usually disappears entirely from a herd following an acute outbreak
    D. may spread from any number of reservoirs in other domestic or wild animals, and does NOT easily lend itself to an eradication program

9. The dose of tuberculin recommended for standard testing is _____ cc.

    A. 0.2   B. 0.5   C. 1.0   D. 0.1

10. To lessen the occasional problem of a retained titer following vaccination with Strain 19 vaccine, it is recommended that animals be vaccinated

    A. following two months of age as soon as possible
    B. between six to ten months of age
    C. either subcutaneously or intradermally
    D. with two injections any time during the gestation period

11. A suspicious brucellosis milk ring test is

    A. presumptive evidence of brucellosis in a herd
    B. right in half of the cases
    C. conclusive evidence of brucellosis in a herd
    D. disregarded unless the intensity of the reaction is at LEAST four plus

12. A bovine animal which was officially vaccinated against brucellosis as a calf is 37 months of age when tested. The blood serum agglutination test reveals complete agglutination at the dilution of one to one hundred.
    The animal is classed

    A. suspect
    B. reactor
    C. negative because the animal was too young to be tested
    D. negative

13. The major cause of condemnations of poultry at time of slaughter in the United States is

    A. avian tuberculosis and Newcastle disease
    B. salmonellosis and fowl plague
    C. mycoplasmosis and leukosis
    D. infectious laryngotracheitis and ornithosis

14. Blood samples to be tested for brucellosis should be

A. held at room temperature pending shipment to the laboratory
B. held at room temperature pending formation of the clot, then refrigerated if necessary pending shipment, but forwarded to the laboratory as soon as possible
C. held at room temperature pending formation of the clot, then frozen prior to forwarding to the laboratory
D. refrigerated until a clot is firm, the clot being removed and discarded, and the serum forwarded to the laboratory within a few days

15. When exposure to scrapie is suspected, periodic inspections of sheep should continue after the date of last exposure for   15.____

    A. six months
    B. two weeks
    C. forty-two months or longer
    D. two months

16. The market cattle identification program is MOST valuable for   16.____

    A. eliminating the need for health certificates
    B. detecting herds of cattle likely to be affected with brucellosis or tuberculosis
    C. determining the incidence of brucellosis and tuberculosis within a given marketing area
    D. removing infected animals from interstate commerce

17. Brain tissue submitted to a laboratory for hog cholera examination should be   17.____

    A. preserved by refrigeration
    B. placed in sterile saline solution to keep the tissue from drying
    C. frozen
    D. shipped in 10% formalin

18. As an accredited veterinarian, you may be called upon to give advice to a client concerning brucellosis infection in his herd.   18.____
    Which of the following would NOT be sound advice?

    A. Retest the infected herd promptly as scheduled
    B. Vaccinate pregnant heifers with Strain 19 vaccine
    C. Isolate any reactors away from the herd until they are disposed of for slaughter
    D. Maintain a constant lookout for any evidence of reproductive problems in breeding animals

19. Twenty export cattle, having met applicable export requirements, are enroute from the state of origin to the port of embarkation.   19.____
    Three calves are born during the trip.
    Which of the following statements is true?

    A. Since the number at origin and number arriving at port of embarkation are different, the entire group MUST be tuberculin tested
    B. No further testing is necessary
    C. The three dams and their calves MUST be tuberculin tested
    D. A negative tuberculin test is necessary for the three calves

20. A state-federal hog cholera eradication program   20.____

    A. has been underway since the discovery of hog cholera
    B. will be underway within 5 years

C. is now underway in the United States
D. is regarded by MOST authorities as being an impossibility

21. Brucellosis in swine may be MOST effectively dealt with by

    A. marketing the entire herd for slaughter as soon as practicable, cleaning and disinfecting the premises, and restocking after sixty days with swine from validated brucellosis-free herds
    B. blood testing the herd at 30 day intervals, eliminating all reactors, and vaccinating the negative females
    C. discontinuing raising pigs for a year, and purchasing feeders as needed to effectively utilize the available feed
    D. isolating all infected animals, and feeding antibiotics until the organisms can no longer be recovered

22. Sheep or cattle scabies infected flocks or herds should be

    A. dipped twice 10 to 14 days apart
    B. dipped once and reinspected after 60 days
    C. sold for slaughter immediately
    D. held in quarantine until the flock or herd is sprayed twice, 10 to 14 days apart

23. Dourine is a reportable disease

    A. of the genital tract of cattle, sheep and goats
    B. diagnosed by the complement-fixation test
    C. affecting ALL grazing animals, caused by the poisonous plant durra
    D. spread by coitus among cattle

24. Which of the following should be remembered in inspecting sheep or cattle for scabies?

    A. If the flock or herd was affected in the spring, but cleared up during the summer, it could NOT be scabies
    B. Report ALL suspicious and positive cases to the animal health officials
    C. If fleece or hair loss is slight, it CANNOT be scabies
    D. Raise scabs at center of denuded area for the presence of mites

25. The test procedure that should be used to diagnose Mycoplasma gallisepticum infected flocks of poultry is

    A. the complement-fixation test
    B. isolation and identification of the virus
    C. the indirect complement-fixation test
    D. the agglutination test plus hemagglutination inhibition for confirmation when needed

KEY (CORRECT ANSWERS)

1. A
2. A
3. A
4. D
5. A

6. B
7. C
8. D
9. D
10. A

11. A
12. A
13. C
14. B
15. C

16. B
17. D
18. B
19. B
20. C

21. A
22. A
23. B
24. B
25. D

TEST 2

DIRECTIONS: Each question or incomplete statement is followed by several suggested answers or completions. Select the one that BEST answers the question or completes the statement. *PRINT THE LETTER OF THE CORRECT ANSWER IN THE SPACE AT THE RIGHT.*

1. A cow at a slaughterhouse with antemortem signs of milk fever should be   1._____

    A. condemned and tanked
    B. treated with calcium and returned in 10 days
    C. treated as a suspect and slaughtered at the end of the day
    D. slaughtered normally

2. What is true of the hog cholera eradication program?   2._____

    A. Reduced incidence of the disease
    B. No vaccination or decreased incidence due to the vaccine
    C. Immediate slaughter follows any outbreak
    D. All of the above

3. A major cause of condemnation of young poultry is   3._____

    A. Newcastle's disease
    B. chronic respiratory disease
    C. leukosis
    D. septicemia

4. The estimated annual losses to livestock owners of the United States from infectious and communicable diseases of animals is   4._____

    A. 100,000,000   B. 500,000,000
    C. 1,000,000,000   D. 10,000,000,000

5. One disadvantage to using inactivated vaccines against hog cholera is that they   5._____

    A. do NOT give immediate protection
    B. CANNOT be used on pregnant sows
    C. require special handling
    D. CANNOT be used if the hogs are to be shipped interstate

6. It is NOT a responsibility of an accredited veterinarian when applying tuberculin tests to   6._____

    A. use technical skill in application and interpretation of the tests
    B. require animals to be restrained when making tests
    C. inform herd owners about disease and program
    D. pass all atypical reactions

7. Which of the following does NOT apply to a tuberculosis-free accredited herd?   7._____

    A. MUST pass a negative test within 15 months from the previous accreditation test to qualify for reaccreditation
    B. The official tuberculin test shall be the intra-dermic test
    C. MUST be tested every 6 months to maintain its status
    D. NO animal that has been designated a reactor at any time shall be retested

8. The poultry industry's annual loss because of poultry diseases is approximately _____ million dollars.

   A. 3 B. 100 C. 200 D. 300

9. In controlled experiments and extensive field surveys, Strain 19 brucella vaccine has been demonstrated to have value in protecting cattle against brucellosis. Under conditions of average exposure in infected herds, there were

   A. 95 percent *fewer* infected cattle within the vaccinated population than within the nonvaccinated population
   B. 85 percent *fewer* infected cattle within the vaccinated population than within the nonvaccinated population
   C. NO infected cattle at all within the vaccinated population
   D. just as many infected animals within the vaccinated population as within the nonvaccinated population, with NO symptoms of abortion within the former

10. A suspicious brucellosis milk ring test is

    A. right in half of the cases
    B. presumptive evidence of brucellosis in a herd
    C. disregarded unless the intensity of the reaction is at LEAST four plus
    D. most often due to mastitis

11. Three bovine females are intended for export to a country in South America. ALL three animals were officially vaccinated (brucella) as calves but are at an age that requires a blood test to be eligible for export. The blood test (brucellosis) appears as follows

	1-50	1-100	1-200
Animal A	-	I	-
Animal B	-	+	-
Animal C	-	+	I

    A. ALL three animals are eligible for export
    B. NONE are eligible for export
    C. ONLY animal A is eligible for export
    D. ONLY animals A and B are eligible for export

12. A bovine animal which was officially vaccinated against brucellosis as a calf is 37 months of age when tested. The blood serum agglutination test reveals complete agglutination at the dilution of one-hundred.
    The animal is classed

    A. reactor
    B. suspect
    C. negative
    D. negative because the animal was too young to be tested

13. Blood samples to be tested for brucellosis should be

    A. held at room temperature pending shipment to the laboratory
    B. held at room temperature pending formation of the clot, then frozen prior to forwarding to the laboratory

C. held at room temperature pending formation of the clot, then refrigerated if necessary pending shipment, but forwarded to the laboratory as soon as possible
D. refrigerated until the clot is firm, when it should be removed and discarded, and the serum forwarded to the laboratory within a few days

14. When exposure to scrapie is suspected, periodic inspections of sheep should continue for   14._____

   A. two weeks
   B. two months
   C. six months
   D. forty-two months or longer

15. The market cattle testing program is MOST valuable for   15._____

   A. determining the incidence of brucellosis within a given marketing area
   B. removing infected animals from interstate commerce
   C. detecting herds of cattle likely to be affected with brucellosis
   D. eliminating the need for health certificates

16. Sorologically, you would classify the standard test for brucellosis as a(n) _____ test.   16._____

   A. precipitin   B. agglutination
   C. inhibition   D. complement fixation

17. One hundred head of cattle are at the Mexican border awaiting importation into the United States. ALL of the animals have been given necessary veterinary inspections, however, fever ticks were discovered on several animals.
The   17._____

   A. animals are permitted entry
   B. entire group MUST be immediately reinspected to see if any ticks were overlooked
   C. fever tick infested animals MUST be removed from the group
   D. animals are ineligible for entry at this time

18. Which of the following should be remembered in inspecting sheep for scabies?   18._____

   A. Raise scabs in the center of the denuded area to check for the presence of mites
   B. If fleece loss is slight, it CANNOT be scabies
   C. If the flock was affected in the spring but cleared up during the summer, it could NOT be scabies
   D. Use a hand lens when examining skin scrapings, and report all suspicious and positive cases to the livestock sanitary officials

19. The tagging procedures for animal identification on tests is to tag   19._____

   A. ALL with official tags
   B. ALL with official tags and record any other identifications
   C. ones WITHOUT any identification and record the identification of others
   D. ALL animals

20. For the purpose of exporting sheep destined to Canada

   A. an accredited veterinarian MUST make physical health examinations and issue health certificates
   B. the health certificates need NOT be endorsed by an authorized Agricultural Research Service veterinarian
   C. an ARS veterinarian MUST make the physical health inspection and issue the health certificates
   D. an accredited veterinarian need only make a physical health examination

21. The disposition of a swine carcass affected with arthritis in both carpal and tarsal joints is to

   A. pass it
   B. pass it for cooking after trimming affected parts
   C. condemn it
   D. condemn and tank the head and pass the rest

22. The BEST test for determination of the presence of horse meat in raw beef sausage is the _____ test.

   A. C-F
   B. anaphylactic
   C. allergy
   D. precipitation

23. On antemortem examination, a hog with a temperature of 106° or MORE should be

   A. passed for food
   B. passed for cooking only
   C. slaughtered as suspect
   D. condemned and tanked

24. Active rancidity in meats is associated with the

   A. mycrolytic bonds between glycerin and fatty acids
   B. slimy condition of the surface of meats
   C. natural proteolytic enzymes present in meats
   D. unsaturated bonds in the long-chain fatty acids

25. According to the standard methods for the examination of dairy products, the BEST practical test to determine the presence of brucella infections in dairy herds is the

   A. bacteriophage typing method
   B. rapid agglutination test on milk serum
   C. milk ring test
   D. cultural and direct microscopic examination

KEY (CORRECT ANSWERS)

1. A
2. D
3. C
4. C
5. A
6. D
7. D
8. D
9. A
10. B
11. B
12. B
13. C
14. D
15. C
16. B
17. D
18. D
19. B
20. C
21. B
22. D
23. D
24. D
25. C

EXAMINATION SECTION
TEST 1

DIRECTIONS: Each question or incomplete statement is followed by several suggested answers or completions. Select the one that BEST answers the question or completes the statement. *PRINT THE LETTER OF THE CORRECT ANSWER IN THE SPACE AT THE RIGHT.*

1. The laboratory test that is MOST accurate in determining the efficiency of pasteurization is

    A. phosphorylase
    B. the standard plate test
    C. the coliform count
    D. the CF test

    1.____

2. You ate some canned ham with NO effect. You reheated the remaining ham the following evening. 6-8 hours later you got nausia and diarrhea as well as other symptoms.
   This is MOST likely _____ food poisoning.

    A. staphylococcus   B. streptococcus
    C. salmonella   D. klebsiella

    2.____

3. To dispose of a cow carcass with eosinophilic myositis you MUST

    A. condemn the entire carcass
    B. pass it for cooking
    C. remove lesions and pass the remainder of the carcass unrestricted
    D. pass the head and condemn the rest

    3.____

4. Pasteurization of milk

    A. kills all bacteria
    B. kills all pathogenic bacteria
    C. reduces the number of all bacteria
    D. reduces the number of pathogenic bacteria to a safer level

    4.____

5. If a person is bitten by a dog it is BEST to

    A. kill the dog and examine the brain for evidence of rabies
    B. keep the dog under observation for rabies
    C. examine the saliva of the dog for evidence of rabies
    D. take NO precautions

    5.____

6. The usual pressure of steam sterilization is _____ pounds.

    A. 2.75   B. 1   C. 15   D. 7.2

    6.____

7. Serum is BEST sterilized

    A. in an autoclave
    B. flowing stream
    C. by filtration
    D. by heating to an appropriate temperature

    7.____

8. The coliform count in pasteurized milk *usually* indicates

   A. contamination after pasteurization
   B. contamination prior to pasteurization
   C. poor pasteurization
   D. none of the above

9. A container of pasteurized milk was found positive to the coliform test. The MOST likely cause is

   A. a contaminated water supply
   B. a broken bathroom steel
   C. improper time or temperature of pasteurization
   D. post-pasteurization contamination

10. Boiling a can of vegetables in anticipation of eliminating the possibility of botulism

    A. will prolong the shelf-life
    B. kills the organism
    C. alters the harmful toxin to a harmless toxin
    D. kills the toxin

11. The proper way to send porcine brain to the diagnostic lab for tests is

    A. refrigerated
    B. frozen
    C. in 10% formalin
    D. in saline suspension

12. An animal that has been designated a reactor to the tuberculin test

    A. may be retested in 60 days by the accredited veterinarian
    B. may be isolated and retested by a regularly employed state or federal veterinarian
    C. MUST be tagged and branded and promptly removed from the herd
    D. should be kept until the calf is weaned

13. For effective disinfection, a 1% solution of sodium orthopenylphena should be applied at

    A. a temperature of 60 degrees F or *higher* and preceded by cleaning with lye
    B. a temperature at or *below* 60 degrees F preceded by cleaning with *highly* alkaline solutions
    C. a temperature at or *above* 60 degrees F NOT preceded by cleaning with *highly* alkaline solutions
    D. 120 degrees F and mixed with sodium hydroxide solution

14. Three head of purebred dairy heifers originating on a farm near St. Louis, Missouri are to be exported to Haiti.
    Which of the following statements is true?

    A. These animals may be exported to Haiti by air from St. Louis after proper veterinary inspection and issuance and endorsement of proper health certificates
    B. These animals must be moved from the premises of origin in cleaned and disinfected conveyances if such conveyances previously were used to haul livestock
    C. The conveyances need not be cleaned and disinfected when moved from the premises of origin under government seal provided vehicle is leak-proof
    D. All of the above statements are correct

15. Tissues submitted to a laboratory for histopathological examination should be

    A. preserved by refrigeration
    B. placed in sterile saline solution to keep the tissue from drying
    C. fixed in a preservative with 10 times as much fixing fluid as tissue
    D. shipped in buffered glycerine

16. Vesicular conditions and other animal diseases NOT readily recognized or easily diagnosed should be reported to state and federal livestock sanitary officials promptly and without fail because

    A. increased world traffic by air and surface routes is multiplying the danger of foreign animal diseases entering the country
    B. of international tension, there is danger that animal diseases will be used as a method of biological warfare
    C. it is necessary to test the efficiency of state-federal emergency disease eradication organizations
    D. indemnity money may be available

17. When scrapie is suspected, the MOST important procedure to follow is to

    A. treat the sheep symptomatically
    B. recommend immediate slaughter of infected animals
    C. report it immediately to state or federal livestock sanitary officials
    D. cull and ship for slaughter

18. Beef products may be imported into the U.S. from a country infested with foot and mouth disease without restriction if

    A. the animals from which the product is derived are vaccinated
    B. effective and acceptable processing has been done in the country of origin
    C. the shipment is moved *directly* to the port of entry
    D. the product is in tight containers

19. Anaplasmosis, an infectious and transmissible disease of cattle characterized by destruction of the erythrocytes

    A. is an example of another livestock disease that has been eradicated from the United States by the efforts of accredited veterinarians and cooperating state and federal regulatory officials
    B. has been reported in a majority of the states and movement of infected animals is subject to state and federal restrictions
    C. has shown no response to broad-spectrum antibiotic treatment
    D. has been kept out of the United States by prompt application of control measures in the Hawaiian Islands in 1955

20. How may animals be certified by an accredited veterinarian for movement from an area of seasonal screwworm infestation into a free area?

    A. By a special screwworm health certificate
    B. On a regular health certificate, following examinations, with the certification that the animals are free of screwworms

C. Without a health certificate, but with a visual inspection 36 hours prior to movement
D. There are NO specific requirements

21. For effective disinfection, a 1% solution of sodium orthophenylphenate should be applied at

    A. a temperature at or *above* 60° F not preceded by cleaning with highly alkaline solutions
    B. a temperature at or *below* 60° F preceded by cleaning with highly alkaline solutions
    C. a temperature of 60° F or *above* and preceded by cleaning with lye
    D. 120° F and mixed with sodium hydroxide solution

22. Disinfection

    A. is the mechanical destruction of pathogenic organisms
    B. MUST be followed by effective cleaning
    C. is the chemical destruction of pathogenic organisms through contact
    D. is achieved in the presence of organic matter

23. Canned ham says, *perishable, keep refrigerated.* This means that

    A. its all right to leave the ham out as long as it does not get warmer than room temperature
    B. the ham has been kept at a plant for 10 days to check its stability
    C. the ham is pasteurized
    D. you must thoroughly cook the meat to avoid a chance of trichina infection

24. The time-temperature relationship of pasteurization is MOST concerned with

    A. killing milk borne pathogens
    B. delaying spoilage
    C. killing all pathogens
    D. removing reductase

25. The absence of phosphatase in milk indicates

    A. improper sterilization
    B. the milk has not been pasteurized
    C. the milk has been pasteurized
    D. the presense of staphlococcus in mastitic milk

KEY (CORRECT ANSWERS)

1.	A	11.	C
2.	A	12.	C
3.	C	13.	C
4.	B	14.	B
5.	B	15.	C
6.	C	16.	A
7.	C	17.	C
8.	A	18.	B
9.	D	19.	B
10.	C	20.	B

21. A
22. C
23. A
24. A
25. C

TEST 2

DIRECTIONS: Each question or incomplete statement is followed by several suggested answers or completions. Select the one that BEST answers the question or completes the statement. *PRINT THE LETTER OF THE CORRECT ANSWER IN THE SPACE AT THE RIGHT.*

1. The principal method employed by MOST meat inspection systems in the U.S. to reduce human trichinosis is to

    A. educate the public to avoid eating raw or semicooked pork products
    B. require the killing of trichina larvae in pork products customarily eaten without further cooking
    C. require the cooking of all garbage fed to swine
    D. require the freezing of all raw pork used in sausage
    E. detect pork carcasses with trichina larvae by microscopic examination of musculature

1.____

2. The modern trend in the milk industry to keep the milk longer under refrigeration on the farm and in the plant and to *decrease* the number of deliveries to the consumers has been *increased* by the importance of _____ bacteria.

    A. thermophilic   B. thermodermic
    C. pathogenic   D. coliform
    E. psychrophilic

2.____

3. Proper pasteurization of milk requires 161° at _____ seconds.

    A. 5   B. 10   C. 12   D. 15   E. 25

3.____

4. In a high temperature short-time pasteurizer in which ALL milk and heating and cooling liquids are closed to the atmosphere, the milk pump may be located between the

    A. raw milk side of the regenerator and the heater
    B. heater and the holder
    C. holder and the hot milk side of the regenerator
    D. regenerator and the cooler
    E. cooler and the bottler

4.____

5. Many diseases pass meat inspection because there are NO visible lesions, although they should be condemned.
The condition that is NOT like this is

    A. leukemia (lymphosarcoma)
    B. tetanus
    C. milk fever
    D. railroad sickness
    E. rabies

5.____

6. Before fresh pork can leave an inspected establishment, it

    A. need not be treated in any way to kill trichina
    B. must be heated to an internal temp, of 137°
    C. must be heated to an internal temp of 145°

6.____

D. can be used only for processed products
E. must bear recommended cooking instructions

7. The minimum treatment with steam under pressure by which large bundles of surgical equipment can be completely sterilized is _____ minutes.

   A. 212° F for 15
   B. 212° F for 30
   C. 225° F for 30
   D. 250° F for 15
   E. 250° F for 30

8. The organism that is MOST likely to be found in pasteurized milk is

   A. brucella
   B. lactobacillus dermaphilus
   C. staphlococcus
   D. strep. lactus
   E. anthrax

9. Certified milk must NOT contain a bacterial count of MORE than

   A. 1,000
   B. 10,000
   C. 20,000
   D. 50,000
   E. 5,000,000

10. To protect yourself from the destructive effects of the x-ray during fluoroscopy you should

    A. wear a lead apron and lead gloves
    B. stand behind the control panel
    C. wear a film badge that will warn you against excess radiation
    D. wear fluoroscopic goggles
    E. wear heavy clothing

11. A vat of milk is held at 72°F for several hours prior to pasteurization and being made into cheese.
    An outbreak of food poisoning in persons consuming the cheese is probably due to

    A. E. coli
    B. strep. ag.
    C. aerobacter
    D. salmonella spp.
    E. staph aureus

12. Milk becomes rancid as a result of

    A. an *increase* in sediment
    B. lipase activity
    C. slow cooling
    D. an *increase* in leukocyte content
    E. coliform contamination

13. The U.S. Public Health service milk ordinance and code requires that Grade A pasteurized milk MUST have a bacteria count per ml of NOT more than

    A. 30,000 by *direct* microscopic count and a coliform count of 0
    B. 30,000 by *direct* microscopic count and a coliform count of not more than 10
    C. 20,000 by *plate* count and a coliform count of not more than 10
    D. 50,000 by *plate* count and a coliform count of not more than 10
    E. 50,000 by *direct* microscopic count and a coliform count of not more than 10

14. After a nuclear attack, poultry may represent one of the MOST dependable sources of fresh food of animal origin because

    A. they do not as a rule eat the vegetation likely to be exposed to fallout
    B. they present a small surface for the absorption of fallout
    C. they are the most radioresistant species of domesticated animals
    D. their roosting habits protect them against fallout
    E. their feathers protect them against contamination

15. A smoked ham is prepared and a portion of it consumed without ill effects. The next day the leftover part is heated to a boiling temperature for a few minutes and then served. The persons who eat the ham become ill 6 to 8 hours later. Their symptoms are nausea, vomiting, diarrhea, abdominal cramps, headache, and sweating. They recover within 25 hours.
    This type of food poisoning is MOST likely

    A. streptococcal   B. ptomaine
    C. staphlococcal   D. chemical
    E. salmonella

16. A process along with sanitation that has helped to prevent bone sour in cured hams is

    A. freezing before curing   B. dry curing
    C. vein pumping   D. soaking hams
    E. smoking hams

17. The *minimum* temperature at which meat affected with trichinosis must be heated is _____ degress F.

    A. 60-70   B. 70-80   C. 80-90
    D. 90-100   E. *greater* than 137

18. An enzyme that is a normal constituent of milk and is used in a laboratory test to check the efficiency of pasteurization is

    A. phosphatase   B. peroxidase   C. reductase
    D. calactase   E. lipase

19. Some conditions require condemnation of the whole carcass yet on autopsy, very few or no lesions are noted.
    One such condition is

    A. rabies   B. hog cholera   C. milk fever
    D. tetanus   E. TB

20. On post mortem, you are presented with a porcine carcass that has diamond shaped lesions mostly on the back. These lesions are about one inch long and 1/4 inch in diameter. Careful examination reveals no other lesions. The MOST recent USDA regulations recommend to

    A. condemn the whole carcass
    B. condemn the skin and pass the rest of the carcass
    C. condemn the skin and pass the carcass for cooking
    D. pass the whole carcass
    E. condemn the head and pass the rest

KEY (CORRECT ANSWERS)

1. B
2. E
3. D
4. A
5. A

6. E
7. E
8. B
9. A
10. A

11. E
12. B
13. C
14. C
15. C

16. A
17. E
18. A
19. C
20. B

www.ingramcontent.com/pod-product-compliance
Lightning Source LLC
Chambersburg PA
CBHW082213300426
44117CB00016B/2788